COLLECTOR'S GUIDE TO
ROCKINGHAM
THE ENDURING WARE
IDENTIFICATION & VALUES

MARY BREWER

COLLECTOR BOOKS
A Division of Schroeder Publishing Co., Inc.

Searching For A Publisher ?

We are always looking for knowledgeable people considered experts within their fields. If you feel that there is a real need for a book on your collectible subject and have a large comprehensive collection, contact us.

Book design: Karen Geary
Cover design: Beth Summers

Additional copies of this book may be ordered from:

Collector Books
P.O. Box 3009
Paducah, Kentucky 42002-3009

@ $14.95. Add $2.00 for postage and handling.

Copyright: Mary Brewer, 1996

Printed by IMAGE GRAPHICS, INC., Paducah, Kentucky

DEDICATION

To two lovely women, my late mother, Helen Herring, who first introduced me to the joys of collecting, not only for the appreciation of the object itself, but for the sense of history it could impart; and to her dear friend, and mine, Glenadine Larsen, who has continued to share this interest with encouragement and love.

ACKNOWLEDGMENTS

As in any of life's endeavors, the completion of this book was not accomplished in a vacuum, but through the encouragement of my family and friends. John Brewer, aided and abetted me in the quest for new and different pieces of Rockingham, inspired me to search for information about our collection, and learn about the history of the ware. Happily, he lived to read the letter of interest from my publisher. If it were not for the inspiration, generosity, and help of a special friend, Susan Henke, my few pieces of Rockingham would never have become a collection.

I must also acknowledge the patience of Rob Donnelly of Picture This, who directed me toward better and better photographs. A thank you also goes to Virpi Soderberg, who assisted me on my travels photographing museum pieces.

My appreciation goes to Harold Hamilton and Missouri Representative Ken Fiebelman who have shared pieces from their collections and shops.

Lastly, my gratitude goes to the staffs of the Newark Museum and to the Museum of Ceramics. Without their direction to proper information, the knowledge which became the basis for this book would not have been acquired.

CONTENTS

INTRODUCTION

It has been quoted, there is nothing new under the sun, and as I gathered the material for this book, these words repeated themselves to me over and over again. Without the material previously published, much of it now out of print; without the information from real experts, the curators of our museum; without the knowledge of collectors and dealers, this information would have been impossible to compile.

Recognizing this, my goal in this book is to reintroduce information about Rockingham ware which has, for most collectors, been difficult to find. With the examples of many of the plates I hope further, to eliminate misconceptions, some of which have been around for years. It is also my hope that we can use this information to help us make informed choices for the boundaries of our collections, large or small. To become well informed collectors we must first understand what Rockingham is, and what it is not.

In addition to the compiled information, we must keep in mind that the vast majority of Rockingham ware was not made to decorate a shelf, but to be used in everyday food preparation or food service in the home. With this in mind I remembered a wonderful exhibit at the Museum of American Folk Art in New York where the vessels for food preparation and old-time recipes were gathered together in a delightful presentation. It was this exhibition which inspired me to search through our collection of family recipes, receipts as my grandmother called them, for special ones I might include in this book. We have been a family of cooks for many generations so some of these recipes date to the 1800s, and except for the directions for the pigeon pie, I've tried them all.

HOW COLLECTIONS
ARE BORN

The round bowl in front of me was the color of coffee streaked with butterscotch, an unlikely combination, but to my young eyes it was beautiful. I was waiting for my mother, a glass collector, who was browsing in her favorite antique shop in Bend, Oregon. The elderly shop owner, seeing my interest, came over to the table where I was standing and said, "That's Bennington. It's from Vermont." She had the last part partially right, the wonderful bowl could have been from Vermont.

As Barret said in his book on the Bennington potteries, "the city of Bennington is to pottery what Sandwich, Massachusetts, is to glass." While the Bennington potteries produced different kinds of ceramics, their output of Rockingham ware was so great, especially from the pottery owned by C. W. Fenton, that the town name of Bennington became synonymous with Rockingham ware. But, using the word Bennington, as was done when as a girl I saw my first piece, was incorrect. I could have been told correctly, "It's a Rockingham bowl." If it has an appropriate mark, she could have said, "It's a Bennington Rockingham bowl," and then she could have gone on describing who made the brown glazed bowl.

Years later, my mother-in-law gave me a brown bowl and the only remaining custard of a set of six. The bowl and custard set had been a 1925 wedding gift to her in Medford, Oregon. Much lighter in color than the first piece I saw, these pieces had a golden brown glaze over a yellow ware body. With this gift I was hooked, and a collection was born. (Plate 1)

My curiosity was aroused, the pieces I

Plate 1

had seen were very different from each other. With little money, but lots of interest, I began searching for information about this ware. When I asked dealers, I received conflicting information, and it wasn't until several years later as I sat down next to a dealer at an auction, that I was given clear direction. This kind man began my education, explaining the pitcher I was waiting to bid on was not Bennington. "It's properly called Rockingham ware," he told me. "Get Barret's book from the library, it will help you understand." That book, which I now own, gave me the first factual information, and the plates, even though most were in black and white, were even more educational.

Although I was beginning to learn, some of the information given to me was not correct. More than once I was told by someone who was supposed to be an expert, "The light colored pieces are Rockingham, the dark ones are Bennington." By then, with the information from Barret's book I knew this statement was not true.

Today, even though there are to my knowledge no books on Rockingham in print, many collectors' guides for other popularly collected wares, spongeware and yellowware, and collectors' books about specific pottery companies, touch briefly on information about Rockingham. And here another misconception arises. While the authors are experts in their own field of collecting, it's very difficult to be knowledgeable about everything. I was recently told, "Rockingham is just a piece of yellowware with a manganese glaze." This statement is not true.

While it can be said with truth, much of the Rockingham ware was produced on a yellow clay base, not all pieces were made in this way. Many pieces of Rockingham ware were produced from a stoneware clay base. And here rises another misconception. Some have said, "You can always tell a stoneware piece. They're the plain pieces without decoration."

It is a known fact that yellow clay is much more ductile, more easily worked than the coarser stoneware clay. But, early in the 1800s there were fine potters, many of them trained in England, working here in the United States. These men had the skills necessary to produce embossed wares from the stoneware clay. (Plate 2) The anchor-decorated buff stoneware

Plate 2   pitcher with a rich brown Rocking-

8

ham glaze was made by J. Mayer at his Arsenal Pottery in Trenton, New Jersey, c.1860.

An anomaly we see pictured in collectors' guides, and I have seen several pieces offered for sale in shops, is a slip banded yellowware bowl overglazed with Rockingham glaze. (Plate 3) There seems to be no definitive explanation for these. Some authors have proposed that potteries with an unsold inventory of slip decorated yellow-ware, added the Rockingham glaze in hopes of selling it. (Plate 4) The Rockingham turks head mold might have been produced in the same way, in an attempt to make an unpopular item sell. After Rockingham appeared on the market, the earlier red-

Plate 3

Plate 4

ware became difficult to sell because it was much more fragile. Housewives soon learned to prefer Rockingham, a more durable ware, in their kitchens. The wear on the bottom of this piece clearly shows the redware body below the glaze giving us proof that Rockingham glaze was also used on a redware base. But, to do this the red body was first covered by a yellow glaze, then the Rockingham glaze. In addition to the color of the clay body of this piece, it is very light in weight, indicating again, the common redware underneath.

Although we know without doubt from the amount of Rockingham ware we see today, most of it was made on a yellow clay base, these pieces I've described, while not as common, certainly dispute the theory that all Rockingham is yellowware.

WHO MADE IT?

What we now call Rockingham ware was first made in England about 1785 by the Swinton Pottery in Yorkshire. They made complete dinner sets and embellished the pieces with gilt, calling it Brown China. It was produced by the Swinton works until it closed in 1842. The brown glazed ware was named Rockingham by Bingley, the owner, after his patron, the Marquis of Rockingham who had helped him out of numerous serious financial difficulties. Similar to the pottery production in this country, the early English glazes varied from a golden butterscotch color to a dark molasses brown depending on the consistency of the glaze itself and the amount of times the piece was dipped. Some of these early wares showed a controlled streakiness, a design feature which would last into the 1800s. (Plate 5) The Bingley pottery business was sold to the Bramelds and it was under this ownership that the glaze was perfected. Soon Brameld's glaze was copied and by 1826 Rockingham ware was made by Josiah Spode, Copeland, and Garrett in Staffordshire. We also know that the firm of Josiah Wedgewood & Sons was making pieces of Rockingham by 1840. The two marked Rockingham spittoons (Plate 6) from the East Liverpool Ceramics Museum, Ohio, Collection were made in England.

Plate 5

Plate 6

As this new ware grew in popularity, potteries in other countries began making Rockingham. Found in a refuse dig in West Yorkshire, the small individual creamer (Plate 7) was made by the Port Dundas Pottery Co. in Glasgow, Scotland, c.1870. The oval pottery mark is impressed in the stoneware base. The finely made dessert plate (Plate 8) was made in France by the firm of Hautin & Boulanger, c.1880.

In this country, David Henderson of the Jersey City Pottery, in New Jersey, is credited with making the first piece of Rockingham early in the 1820s. After this initial introduction, by about 1835, every sizable pottery in the United States was making the ware.

Plate 7

The glaze for Rockingham ware was made of a mixture of flint, feldspar, red lead or iron oxides, and clay. The brown color was achieved by the addition of a small amount of manganese. After the bisque firing, the piece was either completely dipped, or partially dipped, spattered, or brushed with the glaze. And it appears that by the early 1900s some potters were using a sponge to apply the glaze.

Plate 8

11

Plate 9　　　　　　　　Plate 10

Here is an area of dispute, and when we try to determine a parameter accepted by the manufacturing pottery to clarify it, we reach a dead end. There is a fine line, sometimes only a matter of judgment, between later pieces of Rockingham that were made by thickly sponging on the glaze and spongeware pieces which were made by applying the glaze more lightly, with a dryer sponge. The problem arises because of how spongeware was made and sold. Like Rockingham, it was made on different clay bodies, whiteware, yellowware, and stoneware. Unlike Rockingham ware it was not advertised by its name, spongeware, by the manufacturer, but as stoneware, yellowware, or whiteware. Because of this lack of direction from research material we must use our own judgment with discretion. The pudding bowls (Plate 9) are unquestionably spongeware, but the designation of the wedding gift bowl and custard (Plate 1) is not as clear. Nor is there clear categorization of the stoneware mug. (Plate 10). This piece has been included as an illustration of spongeware in a collector book, but the piece was sold by a knowledgeable dealer as Rockingham. A peacock design pitcher with a glaze similar to this (Plate 11) is described by the Museum of Ceramics in Ohio as light glaze clarifying, I believe, the dilemma. With this expert direction, even though the differences are small between some of the Rockingham with a light glaze and late items such as the spongeware pudding bowls, we see that many pieces

Plate 11

formerly designated as spongeware were not. They were sold by the manufacturer as Rockingham and armed with this knowledge our individual judgments become more informed. Now personal taste, or preference must rule. Personally, I think a few pieces of spongeware complement a collection of Rockingham and if you like to use your antiques as I do, the addition of the pudding bowls can be used as a practical and inexpensive soup or salad bowl.

Today we seldom see the dark dipped pieces. Some collectors and dealers have called them brownware, similar to the earliest English designation. Even Barber who was a nineteenth century author and is still considered a ceramic authority said the dipped pieces were not Rockingham at all, but brownware. So a controversy developed. We know from English ceramic historians that the ware was called by both names. Barret, a curator of the Vermont museum, indicated in his guide to Bennington Pottery that dipping was the glazing method used at the pottery until 1847, and the ware was sold by the pottery that made it as Rockingham. He questioned how we can, as collectors, dispute what the potter who made the piece or the business which sold it, called it. And again knowledge obtained from the Ceramic Museum in Ohio clarifies the debate as they describe a similar barrel shaped canning jar as Rockingham. (Plate 12)

Plate 12

Plate 13

The existence and knowledge of these dipped pieces leads to another misconception. This one involves the depth of color. While we do know many early pieces were dipped and because of this they appear to us an almost solid dark brown, we cannot say with accuracy that all very dark brown pieces are early. (Plate 13) The mug on the right has a very dark brown glaze yet both were made in this century.

A glazed ware similar in appearance to Rockingham ware was first patented in 1849 by the Fenton Pottery in Bennington, Vermont, and was called Flint Enamel. Flint Enamel was made by first applying a clear glaze to the bisque piece, then adding oxides in addition to manganese. The resulting piece looks very much like Rockingham except is has another color or combination of colors, blue, green, or orange, in addition to brown. By 1852 the Ohio potteries were producing Flint Enamel. Even though it was very popular, it was not a profitable pottery to produce because of the high cost of the additional oxides, the cobalt, and copper. While not nearly as common today as Rockingham, because of the short span of production, if we see a pottery piece as the one on the left with color streaked on it in addition to the brown, we know it is not Rockingham. (Plate 14) The two pitchers were made from the same mold design the one a very darkly glazed Rockingham and the other, Flint Enamel.

Plate 14

If we are to comprehend and understand the great variety of pieces and the range of color found in Rockingham ware, we must eliminate two words from our vocabulary and these two are always and never. If we can forget the hard and fast rules implied by these words, we're well on our way to understanding the variety of this ware.

The amount of glaze on pieces range from those which are almost completely covered by dipping the bisque piece in glaze, showing only the smallest portions of the body, a fine line on an embossed design, a tiny patch of cream or yellow color on a handle or on the rim of the base, to another which appears to have been lightly splattered with a brush of glaze, the yellow body making the predominant color of the piece. (Plate15) And yet another, while not as finely spattered as spatterware, it has obviously not been dipped or brushed, but spattered with glaze. The spatters on the pie plate (Plate 16) have a thickness, raised above the body of the plate which can be easily felt with fingertips. The Bennington Museum in Vermont has on display pieces which are covered with this style of spattered Rockingham glaze.

Plate 15

The colors of Rockingham ware can vary from a black brown glazing which has iridescent purple (the English potters described this iridescence as brownish purple) and some pieces showing blue and green lights to others

Plate 16

which are a lightly glazed pale brown, even lighter than the rich butterscotch color I think is the most beautiful of all. If we visualize all of these graduations of brown, from almost black to very pale brown, and think of the variety of colors of the base clay used which shows through the glaze as buff, yellow, or pumpkin color, and then if we look at the variety of ways the potters applied glaze to the clay, we begin to realize the vast variety of ware we properly lump together under the descriptive name, Rockingham.

NEW JERSEY
POTTERS AND POTTERIES

Along with being credited with the first production of Rockingham, in 1829 David Henderson introduced to the United States a manufacturing method used in England, the use of molds. Using this method, Rockingham ware began to be made in molds, not exclusively on the potter's wheel and the cost of production went down making domestic pottery more affordable.

A piece of pottery was made, and from this a mold was taken. Next the potter took some casts from the mold to determine if any changes needed to be made and how long the mold would last which would determine how many molds would be necessary for production. This introduction to the use of molds transformed our pottery workshops into factories.

David Henderson, a Scotsman, purchased the defunct Jersey Porcelain and Earthenware Company on September 29, 1828, and in partnership with his brother under the firm name of D. & J. Henderson began to successfully make molded pottery pieces. In 1833 he incorporated the business under the name of American Pottery Manufacturing Company, more commonly called the American Pottery Co.

The pottery designs from this company moved forward when Daniel Greatbach came from England in 1838 and joined the firm as chief modeler. Barber said that almost all of the designs of an ornamental nature used by the firm in the years between 1838 and 1849 were made by Greatbach.

The most famous Greatbach design, copied by many potteries as this one from the Ohio Collection of East Liverpool Ceramics Museum, (Plate 17) had to be the hound handled pitcher which was being made in Rockingham ware by 1840. The inspiration for the mold came from an English pitcher, which in turn was

Plate 17

inspired from a continental piece which could have been designed from a hound handled pitcher found in Pompeii. Of interest to us is a pre-Columbia American Indian hound handled pitcher dating to about 1000 A.D. indicating the design was certainly not new, and strangely, came back to its original continental home.

Prior to 1838 when Greatbach joined the firm, D. & J. Henderson produced a Rockingham glazed stoneware pitcher with molded designs showing two hunters and a dog on one side, the end of a rabbit hunt on the other. The glaze on this 1829–33 piece is thin brown on the top graduating to a clear glaze on the bottom. After 1833 the firm made cuspidors decorated with a relief decoration of draped vines, pendants, and rosettes.

During the years Greatbach worked at the pottery they made toby pitchers and an octagonal formed paneled pitcher with relief figures of the apostles under gothic arches. A simple stoneware pitcher with Rockingham glaze over an orange peel like texture was made as well as a hexagonal pitcher with an overall relief design of flower and leaf arabesques. One of their most unique designs was a twelve-sided pitcher decorated with foliated scrolls. The head of a toby emerges from this geometric body. In addition to this wide variety of design Henderson's pottery made coffee and teapots with matching cream pitchers and sugar bowls of the highest quality.

In Woodbridge, the Salamander Works was at one time the largest pottery in New Jersey. Established by two Frenchmen, Michiel Lefoulon and Henry DeCasse, in 1825, later it was incorporated under the Salamander name in 1871. The main products of this pottery were fire brick, sewer pipe, and roof tiles, nothing of interest to us as collectors, but between the years of 1836 and 1842 certain Rockingham glazed stoneware pieces were made. After Lefoulon's death in 1842, DeCasse made Rockingham ware between 1842–67.

Lefoulon of the Salamander Works was awarded a diploma from the American Institute of New York for a beautiful specimen of stoneware in 1836. In 1838 and in 1839 the same institute issued the Salamander Works a silver medal for the best specimens of stoneware.

A hound handled pitcher was also made here, apparently adapted from the Greatbach model. The Rockingham glaze turned to a dark olive brown on the lower body of one pitcher. A lambrequin border above the hunting scene and a grape vine border were the design characteristics of this pitcher. Glaze colors on these stoneware pitchers ranged from the one described above, to a reddish brown, to one described as a rich dark brown and one a chocolate brown. This same design was made in a miniature size.

Other relief designs used on pitchers included one of volunteer firemen pulling a fire engine to a flaming house, with green briars on the neck and a plaited handle, another was made with scrolls and fauns heads evenly arranged on the body below an inverted lambrequin border below the neck, and another shows the body of a side wheel steamboat on each side with green briar vines on the neck and a scroll handle. The green briars are native to New Jersey and the steamboat is thought to be the Sirus which was the first steamship to cross the Atlantic in April of 1838.

A fine toby jug was also made by the Salamander Works. This piece was exhibited in a 1947 pottery show at the Newark Museum and reported in an article "N. J. Pottery rarities in a special Exhibition," the American collector, May 1947. "A toby jug made at this pottery is exhibited for the first time...but the designer of...the toby is obviously some English trained potter whose name is still unknown." The unique detail of this piece is the separateness with which the pitcher is held in the toby's hands. In exquisite miniature the detail is perfect, and it is held out, away from the body, as in life.

In South Amboy the Congress Pottery was built in 1828–29 by John Hancock who made Rockingham ware until 1840. The pottery had other owners until 1849, when Abraham Cadmus purchased the pottery and made Rockingham there until his death in 1857. Cadmus's proprietorship was followed by Joseph Wooten until 1860 and then William A. Allen until the buildings were destroyed by fire in 1861.

But it is the period of Cadmus's ownership which is of interest to Rockingham ware enthusiasts. In the same 1947 New Jersey exhibit an outstanding Rockingham statuette of a reclining bull calf was shown. It was believed the statuette was modeled by Daniel Greatbach, somewhere between the years 1849–51, the period between his leaving the Jersey City pottery and his arrival at Fenton's Vermont pottery. He is listed as a modeler in the Jersey City directories of 1849–51. The statuettes he later made in Vermont are similar to the amount of detail on the New Jersey bull calf.

An apostle cuspidor with Rockingham glaze was made at the Congress Pottery as well as a hound handled pitcher with a relief design of firemen pulling a fire engine in parade below a lambrequin border under the shoulder of the pitcher, and a grape vine design on the neck. Another cylindrical formed pitcher with a high relief decoration of large grape vine leaves and grapes was made in Rockingham as well as a covered cylindrical cookie jar. The jar was designed with eight panels separated by fluting and was finished with two ear handles and a domed shaped lid with a round finial.

The Rockingham output from the Swan Hill Pottery in South Amboy was long and varied. James Carr owned the pottery from 1852–55 and there is a stoneware foot warmer with a fish shaped neck and a tall candlestick from his ownership. We know that during J. L. Rue's tenure, the pottery made a Rockingham toby jug with a different design. The head of the toby rose out of a six paneled jug. Practical items such as buttons and bed warmers were also made here.

In Perth Amboy, W. H. Benton operated the Eagle Pottery between 1858 and 1865. Interesting relief designs of eagles were issued as decoration on different bodied Rockingham pitchers. A pear shaped pitcher was decorated with the American eagle with a shield and thunderbolts on each side. Another pitcher mold was ten sided, but pear shaped with an eagle as decoration. A Greatbach type hunting scene was used as relief decoration on one, and on another a design of acorns and oak leaves was used as decoration. The Rockingham glaze ranged in color from a mottled golden brown to medium dark brown.

Rockingham ware was made at the pottery belonging to A. Hall & Sons in Perth Amboy, after Enoch Wood left Fenton's Bennington pottery 1870–74 and joined this firm. Buff stoneware teapots and pitchers with Rockingham glaze were exhibited at the Newark Museum. Pear shaped pitchers with rustic handles were decorated with relief designs of a running stag on one side and a turkey hanging by its feet on the other. (Plate 18)

Plate 18

The only known marked example of the work of Taylor & Speeler, who operated the Trenton Pottery Company between 1865 and 1872, was a large Rockingham pitcher.

Barber wrote in his book on pottery that J. Mayer made excellent Rockingham wares at the Arsenal Pottery in the 1860s and 1870s. His is the only known New Jersey Rebekah at the Well teapot. The relief design and the legend below was on both sides of the teapot. Mayer also made a darkly colored pear-shaped pitcher with the anchor decoration. (Plate 19) Below the lip is a relief decoration of rope and at the base, front and back a large acanthus leaf, the applied handle partially covers the rear leaf.

While some of these descriptions may seem tedious, this marked Mayer pitcher was found in a Missouri shop in the late 1980s for a very reasonable price. We know that many more pieces of Rockingham ware were made in New Jersey. The constrains of space place limitations, and because of this I have chosen to describe items that can be fully documented by museum archives. I have tried to fully describe these individual pieces in detail because some of them, like the Mayer pitcher purchased in the late 1980s are still to be found.

Plate 19

VERMONT
POTTERS AND POTTERIES

The most famous of all of the New England potteries are the two that made the town name of Bennington synonymous with Rockingham ware. When we think of Bennington Rockingham ware, we are usually referring to the pottery owned by Christopher Webber Fenton during a rather brief period of time between the years 1847 and 1859 when the company collapsed.

The first Bennington pottery was started in 1793, by Captain John Norton. Producing simple jugs, plates, milk pans, and crocks, it wasn't until fifty years later, about 1845, when Norton's grandson Julius Norton formed a partnership with his brother-in-law, Fenton, that Rockingham pottery was made in Bennington. Their partnership lasted until 1847, when Fenton struck out on his own. But during the time of their association, Fenton convinced Norton to expand the pottery's production to include Rockingham. They added, to quote an 1845 sales list, "fancy pitchers and fancy flower pots" to their more mundane offering of beer bottles, churns, pots, jugs, and pudding pots.

Fenton wanted to expand more, to try to produce porcelain. By 1847 he had started a pottery of his own in the north wing of the Norton Pottery, and here Fenton experimented, trying to produce porcelain and the popular designs from the English Staffordshire region.

Even as he moved his pottery to another building where he added two partners, Alanson P. Lyman and Calvin Park, to his firm, he continued to produce Rockingham. In 1848, the firm of Lyman, Fenton & Park advertised Rockingham, but no marked pieces have ever been found from this period. Park left the company in 1849, and the pottery then became known as Lyman, Fenton & Co. Many pieces bear this mark.

In the 1850s the pottery was enlarged with the addition of three kilns in a newly built factory building, and for awhile the firm was managed by Oliver A. Gager, but Fenton kept a minor interest.

Sometime in 1851 Daniel Greatbach joined the pottery as a modeler and pottery designer. The collaboration between the innovative Fenton and the extremely talented and well trained Greatbach produced some delightful wares in Rockingham and flint enamel. (Plate 20) Their working relationship had to have been exciting and fulfilling to both

Plate 20

of these men who delighted in producing ceramics that were on the leading edge of design for their day.

In 1853, under the name of the United States Pottery Company, the company exhibited wares at an exhibition at the Crystal Palace in New York City. A woodcut of their display from Gleason's Pictorial, a Boston paper, of October 22, 1853, shows the huge pillared pottery centerpiece of the exhibit and many of Greatbach's figural designs, regal lions, and supine does in Rockingham amid Rockingham pitchers and cuspidors and other useful items. The woodcut has served as an inventory of the varied production items. The standing stag and the doe illustrated in the woodcut have never been found, but many examples of Greatbach's fine modeling exist, a dairy of Rockingham cows, eight poses and types in all, six poses of Flint Enamel lions, Rockingham poodles with coleslaw topknots, similar in design to the Staffordshire production of the same period must have delighted the onlookers. Recumbant does and stags for mantle decoration; greyhound, lion, and lion head inkwells added to the variety of ware they produced.

Flasks in the shape of boots and books (Plate 21) and bottles in the form of coachmen and toby figures sitting astride barrels, toby snuff jars, the hat is the removable lid, and toby pitchers were all made in Rockingham ware in addition to bowls and pie plates, teapots, coffee pots, mugs and beakers, covered and open serving dishes, (Plate 22) soap dishes, a wide variety of items.

Plate 21

Plate 22

Like most of the potteries, Fenton's company did not mark all of their production. If they had, collecting Rockingham made at Bennington would be far simper. But because of the huge amount of the ware produced, there still are many marked pieces to be found for a price. Thanks to the work of the curators of the Bennington Museum there was much information available to the collector, but those books are now out of print and difficult and costly to find. Because of this I think it is timely to reintroduce some of that information.

Earlier, color and depth of color were mentioned. I want to reiterate that information. Dipping was the glazing method used to produce Rockingham ware from 1841 to at least 1847. Because of this we know the early production was very dark. But, we cannot say that any dark piece of Rockingham is early. We must also look at the design of the piece. By 1849 the Rockingham production at Bennington had become the mottled tortoise shell looking glaze we most commonly associate with the ware today.

The Bennington Rockingham was made in such quantity, so many pieces for every day use, it is difficult to attribute unmarked pieces to this company. But there are known characteristics which help to identify some pieces. The raised supports or pads on the bottom pieces, (Plate 23) were not done at Bennington, nor were the little indentations found on the bottom rims of pie plates or bowls. If you find these marks on the bottom of a piece you know it was not made at Bennington. The Bennington pottery did not make bowls with design

Plate 23

in relief, the bowls and nappies made by Fenton were plain, like the pie plates, inside and out and fully glazed.

The plainness of utilitarian items was made up for in the pieces for the table. Twelve different styles of teapots were made in Rockingham but the Bennington pottery did not made the popular Rebekah at the Well design. They made a tall, 9" high, six paneled teapot with a handle shaped like the number seven and a domed lid with a pointed finial. Five plain pots were made in sizes from 4½" to 7⅝" high. A popular design of alternating ribs was used on two different teapots, one 6½" and another 7⅝" high. The pattern alternated a narrow vertical rib with one twice as wide. Both teapots were made with domed lids with finials and applied scroll decorated handles and spouts. Another alternate rib design decorated the bottom two thirds of a 7½" high teapot, the top of the mold was decorated with acanthus leaves. The lid on this pot was flatter with a round finial. The popular acanthus leaf pattern decorated a 7" high teapot with a rounded lid and pointed finial with a scroll decorated handle and spout.

Of all of the practical table items, there were probably more designs used on pitchers than any other item made in Rockingham. The earliest pitchers had six-sided panel bodies with embossed flowers and leaves in each panel in many different combinations. The alternate rib pattern was used, a tulip and heart, a diamond pattern, a hunting scene, a swirled alternate rib, and a rarely seen pattern with a mask decorated spout. Both bulbous and cylindrical shaped pitchers were made, one a barrel shape, another with Gothic arches, one called sweetheart with a large embossed heart-shaped scroll on both sides of the body and an applied handle that split on the bottom side, leaving a triangular space where the two pieces attached to the body. Two popular paneled designs were acanthus leaf and grapevine, and rarer yet today, a pond lily pattern and another showing Cupid and Psyche.

Daniel Greatbach improved upon his earlier hound handled pitcher design and his design made at Fenton's Pottery was unsuccessfully copied by many companies. There are four distinguishing characteristics to a Greatbach Bennington pitcher. The head of the hound is raised above the pitcher with an arched neck giving room to put your little finger in the space between the forelegs which rest on the top of the pitcher and the bottom of the dog's arched neck. The dog's nose, duck billed in shape, rests on his front paws. The underside of the body of the dog is rough, sharp to the touch, the mold seam was not cleaned smooth. The dog must be wearing a link collar, not a strap. All of these points must be in evidence for a hound handled pitcher to be attributed to the Fenton Pottery. They were referred to as dog handle pitchers in the sale bills and were made in four sizes ranging from 6 quart, 4 quart, and 3 quart, down to 2 quart, the smallest size made.

There was only one design of toby jug made in Bennington. The toby illustrated here (Plate 24) is very close to the Greatbach design, but the bottom of the this same toby (Plate 25) is extremely concave. The bottom of a Bennington toby is almost flat and completely glazed.

Rockingham poodles made at Bennington held a basket of fruit in their mouths and stood on four feet without a base. They were made in pairs facing each other and stood 8" to 9½" tall.

Another figural, yet useful in addition to being decorative, was the cow creamer made at Bennington. Cow creamers were made out of five different materials, including Rockingham. The creamer made by the Fenton pottery has five details which must be evident to classify it as a Benington-made piece. The color must be mottled, not a completely dipped brown creamer. The cow's eyes must be open and the nostrils must be cresent shaped. Additionally there must be well-defined folds in the neck and the ribs. The mold of the Bennington creamer produced cows with such deep folds on the neck and such well defined ribs that they are easily felt with the finger tips. If the piece in question does not have

Plate 24

Plate 25

all of these characteristics, it was made at one of a hundred different potteries here or in England.

The cost of production, the rising costs of cordwood, the huge amount of breakage in shipping over rough roads in horse-drawn wagons were the reasons the company closed its doors on May 15, 1858, also closing an era of accomplishment in ceramic design.

OHIO
POTTERS AND POTTERIES

It has been estimated that between 45% and 65% of the Rockingham produced in this country during the last half of the nineteenth century was produced in Ohio. And the town of East Liverpool, later known as "Crockery City" was the site of most of this production. (Plate 26) The diorama at the East Liverpool Ceramic Museum shows the busy decorating room of a pottery.

Plate 26

Because of the vast clay beds and the river for transportation, East Liverpool prospered producing pottery. It wasn't until the completion of the railroads opening all of the United States market to this Ohio manufacturing center that the pottery industry truly developed. The small Rockingham pitcher (Plate 27) is the type of ware sent by water or rail to markets all over the United States.

Benjamin Harker Sr. came from England in 1839 and bought 50 acres of land just outside of East Liverpool. His purchase was rich

Plate 27

in clay deposits and it is said that James Bennett bought his clay from Harker. Bennett's kiln produced the first Rockingham in East Liverpool. From that modest beginning in 1840, tons of Rockingham ware were produced by many potteries until the firm of D. E. McNicols fired the last kiln in 1927. While the Ohio production of Rockingham did not begin as early as that in Trenton, New Jersey, Ohio's total output was far greater.

The first East Liverpool potter to make Rockingham, James Bennett, was born in Newhall, Burton-on-Trent, in South Derbyshire, England. Initially he worked at potteries in Jersey City, New Jersey, then in Troy, Indiana. Bennett opened the pottery in Ohio in 1839. In 1841 his brothers Edwin, Daniel, and William arrived from England, the first of the skilled potters from the Staffordshire district to come to Ohio. Even though they didn't stay in Ohio long, their pottery was the beginning of Ohio's pottery industry.

Although the Englishman, Benjamin Harker Sr., who bought the clay rich 50 acres outside of East Liverpool in 1839, was not a potter himself, in 1840 he opened the second pottery in this Ohio town. He leased the pottery to Edward Tunnicliff and John Whetton, but the arrangement was not successful and the lease was terminated. Thomas Croxall and John Goodwin, two skilled potters, joined Tunnicliff in 1842. This undertaking also proved unsatisfactory and the agreement was dissolved by mutual consent. Next, Benjamin Harker Sr. hired Goodwin to teach his two sons, Benjamin Jr. and George S. the pottery trade. The sons operated the pottery until 1846, when James Taylor joined the firm and the new business was named Harker, Taylor & Company.

They constructed a three-story brick building which they named "Etruria" after the famous Wedgewood works in England and the new company prospered. By 1848 they were making door knobs and table ware in Rockingham, and in 1850 the firm won a silver medal for its Rockingham production from the Massachusetts Charitable Mechanic Association. Among the award winning pieces of table ware was a hound handled pitcher of exceptional quality.

The skilled English potter, Henry Speeler also worked for the firm, and in 1851 he and Taylor left for Trenton where they would begin their own firm. In this same year, Ezekiel Creighton and Matthew Thompson who provided additional capital and administrative expertise, joined Harker Sr. in partnership and this firm continued producing high quality Rockingham ware. In 1854 Creighton died and the partnership was dissolved. Benjamin Jr. left the firm for a few years but George continued to manufacture Rockingham until he died in

1864. His sons contin-
ued the production of
Rockingham making
decorative and useful
items such as this
cuspidor (Plate 28) until
1879.

Plate 28

John Goodwin, the
potter who first worked
for Bennett, then for
Harker when he came to
the United States from
Burslem, England, in
1842, rented a small pottery in 1843, calling it the Eagle Pottery. Here
he worked for himself and made Rockingham ware.

By 1846 Goodwin enlarged his operation with the purchase of the
Blakely property where he had 20 operatives, potters, working for
him. Rockingham teapots and coffee pots, pitchers and sugars, ewers,
washbowls, and spittoons were manufactured until he sold the business in 1853 and returned to real estate.

Later, in 1872, with his three sons, Goodwin purchased the Broadway Pottery Works and during the next three years again produced
Rockingham. After Goodwin died in 1875, the plant was closed for
seven months, but his sons, Henry, James, and George reopened the
company as the Goodwin Brothers Pottery Company and they continued Rockingham production until about the mid 1800s.

About 1853 another Englishman opened a small pottery where
Rockingham ware was manufactured for a few years. A marked chamber pot in the Museum of Ceramics in East Liverpool has a circular
mark with Richard Harrison impressed around the top of the circle
and East Liverpool Ohio in three lines in the center of the mark.

For a brief but productive period, William Bloor, another skilled
English potter, worked a Rockingham pottery between 1849 and 1855,
then he moved to Trenton.

Between the years 1844 and 1888, Rockingham ware was produced by Thomas Croxall, his father, his younger brothers, and his
partner, James Cartwright. The Union Pottery was purchased in 1856,
and again in 1863 the firm was expanded when Croxall and
Cartwright purchased the Mansion Pottery of Salt and Mear. A two-
story addition was added, and by 1876, this was one of the largest potteries in the East Liverpool area producing fifty to sixty thousand
dollars a year. In 1888 John Croxall acquired Cartwright's interest and

bringing his sons, George and Joseph, into the firm, renamed it J. W. Croxall and Sons. This company continued Rockingham production and in 1892, advertised a full line which included spittoons, bed pans, foot warmers, pitchers, teapots, and covered chambers.

Another native of England from the famous Staffordshire district, James Vodrey, came to East Liverpool after working at potteries in Pennsylvania, Kentucky, and Indiana. In 1848 he formed a partnership with a prosperous farmer, William Woodward, and they produced Rockingham among other wares. The pottery was destroyed by fire in March of 1848, but the partners were given financial support from two businessmen, John and James Blakely. The new partnership was called, Woodward, Blakely, and Company and was appropriately name the Phoenix Pottery. Rockingham was manufactured and in 1852, the firm won a gold medal for its ware from the American Institute. Even though the firm's production was good, they experienced many difficulties, internal disputes, flood damage, and economic hardship from the depressions of the mid 1800s, until the partnership was ended.

Vodrey, with his three sons, converted an empty church into a pottery and by 1858, the Vodrey and Brother Pottery Company was producing Rockingham. Palissy Works was the name the pottery was commonly called during its first years of operation. Vodrey died in 1861, and his son John was killed in the Civil War, but after the war, production was resumed and the firm made Rockingham until 1876.

Among the many pottery firms in the East Liverpool area whose work has not been defined by marks is the pottery belonging to the Larkin Brothers. The reclining girl inkwell (Plate 29) and an accompa-

Plate 29

nying reclining boy inkwell are displayed in the Ceramic Museum Collection in Ohio, and attributed to the Larkin Brothers production of 1848–1861.

When Benjamin Harker Jr. left his father's partnership in 1853, he joined William Smith in a partnership and the two men bought the old Mansion House Pottery once owned by Salt and Mear. (Later, in 1863, the Mansion House Pottery was purchsed by Croxall and Cartwright.) Their 30 employees produced Rockingham until the hard economic times of the mid-1800 depression forced the pottery to close.

Another partnership, that of Isaac Knowles, a cabinet maker by trade and Issac Harvey, began Rockingham production in 1854. Most of their production was fruit jars (Plate 30) like these illustrated, until their product became obsolete when self sealing glass jars were invented in the 1870s. Rockingham production was continued with well designed pieces like their tea kettle (Plate 31) after Knowles brought his son and son-in-law into the firm which became known as Knowles, Taylor & Knowles. The successful production of ironstone resulted in the deletion of the Rockingham ware around 1872.

Plate 30

As with many other pottery families in Ohio, several generations of Brunts worked in East Liverpool. An English potter, William Brunt Sr. formed a partnership with his son-in-law, William Bloor. By the middle of the year 1849, the company was producing Rockingham, but production was short lived, by 1850 the company was producing knobs exclusively. Like many of these small

Plate 31

pottery firms, money was always tight and the lack of sufficient operating capital was usually the cause of financial collapse. A gold strike was responsible for the continued success of this firm. Money was tight and both William Brunt Jr. and William Bloor decided to try their luck in the California gold fields. They hit it rich and came home in 1855 with ten thousand dollars worth of gold dust, the capital the company so desperately needed.

In 1859, William Brunt Jr. left the knob works and bought a section of the old Phoenix Pottery where he produced Rockingham. The Civil War's negative impact was not felt so strongly by this new firm, William Brunt Jr. and Company, after the infusion of capital from the gold dust. A price list from 1865–66 advertised pitchers, spittoons, mugs, pie plates, chamber pots, bowls, bakers, snuff jars, and butter pots. The pottery continued to prosper with an annual total production of nearly fifty thousand dollars worth of earthenware.

Continuing to operate his own firm, Brunt Jr. was also associated with two other potteries. In partnership with his brother Henry and H.R. Hill, he owned the firm of Hill, Brunt, and Company, known as the Great Western Pottery Works, where Rockingham was produced until 1874.

While the Laughlin name is readily associated with the production for semi-vitreous china table ware and their justly famous Fiesta line, when Homer Laughlin first came to East Liverpool following the Civil War, he formed a company with his brother, Shakespeare, that sold Rockingham ware on a wholesale basis.

Three potters, Frederick, Shenkle, and Allen formed a company which later became the Globe Pottery Company in 1888. Both the production of the early firm in 1882 and that of Globe included Rockingham ware.

The company finally known as McNicol, Burton, and Company went through many partnership changes in its development. But Rockingham ware was produced from about 1869 on. The company kept expanding and adding new equipment, and by 1881, the firm was producing three kilns of yellow ware and Rockingham per week. Even after the death of William Burton Sr. in 1881, the company continued operation.

When Daniel Edward McNicol took over the company as president in 1892, the firm was incorporated as the D. E. McNicol Company. Rockingham ware was produced until 1927, making this the last East Liverpool company to produce the ware. Their catalogue advertised bakers, nappies, soap dishes, pie plates, butter jars, bowls, spittoons, mugs, jugs, ale jugs, milk boilers, and pineapple, jewel, octagon, and Rebecca at the Well teapots.

In Roseville, Ohio, the Nelson McCoy Company, well known for its art pottery production, produced a line of Rockingham ware beginning 1916. They named the ware, Nuroc, (new Rockingham) after the old English ware their advertising said. In this line was a mug with a handle which differed from the usual strap handle. The Nuroc mug has an applied ring handle, just large enough for one finger.

Wellsville, Ohio, was the site of the John Patterson and Son Pottery which produced Rockingham ware between the years of 1883 and 1907. Their line included mugs, a soap dish, a humidor, pitchers, nappies, bowls, and a teapot.

In 1904 the Roseville Pottery in Zanesville produced a line of

Plate 32

33

Rockingham ware novelty figures. Of the banks they produced, the most commonly found form is a molded dog's head.

While most Rockingham production consisted of utilitarian items, the firm of John Howson in Zanesville produced decorative Staffordshire type dogs, and book flasks. Among his utilitarian offerings was a toothbrush holder. He even sold an asthma inhaler.

George Pyatt worked in Zanesville for ten years before moving to Missouri in 1859. The number of moves and firm changes made by these early potters gives us a good indication of the marginal profit most of them earned. Many of the pottery businesses were so strapped for operating capital that the smallest economic event could cause financial disaster.

In Cincinnati, George Scott and Son operated a pottery making Rockingham until 1901, and Samuel Pollack and his family owned the Dayton Street Pottery where they made the ware between 1859 and 1874. In addition to the two economic depressions of the early 1800s, the economic impact of the Civil War affected all of these small businesses. M. & N. Tempest originally operated the Dallas Pottery, but by 1864, it was owned by Frederick Dallas who continued Rockingham production until 1869.

One of the most unique and impressive examples of the potter's art is displayed in the Collection of the Ceramic Museum of East Liverpool, Ohio. (Plate 32) The maker of the massive two part umbrella stand is unknown, but not unappreciated.

ANCILLARY
POTTERS AND POTTERIES

Of special interest to Rockingham collectors is the Baltimore, Maryland firm of Edwin Bennett Company. After leaving East Liverpool, Bennett began Rockingham production in Maryland. His brother William joined him from Ohio and stayed for eight years. This firm hired the master modeler Charles Coxon in 1850, and it was while Coxon was working for Bennett that he executed the original design of the Rebecca at the Well teapot. This copy of his design is

unidentified (Plate 33), but the popularity of his creation is attested to by the dozens of firms that copied his design with dozens of varieties of teapots, this copy being only one of many. Other Coxon designs made in Rockingham ware were a toby mug, made by both the Bennett firm and the Swan Hill Pottery in New Jersey, probably while Coxon worked for them. The Bennetts also produced a Rockingham hound handled

Plate 33

pitcher of Coxon's design. While the design is not as well known, he designed a standing stork pitcher. The creative work of this master modeler was still being copied in the production pieces of the D. E. McNicol Pottery in the twentieth century.

The reasons Philadelphia became the pottery center in Pennsylvania were the same as those of East Liverpool, Ohio, and Trenton, New Jersey, good transportation and abundant clay deposits. One of the earliest potters to produce Rockingham was Thomas Haig who made a pitcher design with a full relief of George Washington as a master mason. His sons took over the firm and continued operation until 1890.

Abraham Miller was the son of another early Philadelphia potter, Andrew Miller. After his father's death, Abraham bought out his siblings interest in the firm which became known as the Spring Garden Pottery and continued the production of a line of Rockingham ware until the plant was closed in 1859–60.

The J. E. Jeffords Company is of special interest to collectors because of the firm's chief modeler who worked for them between 1850 and 1868, Stephen Theiss of Bennington. Theiss, a Belgian, designed cow creamers and toby pitchers for the Jeffords Company. He was said to have been the best all round potter when he worked at the Bennington pottery. Of the known Jeffords Pottery production are teapots, bakers, pie plates, and pipkins in Rockingham. And almost all potteries made many unmarked household items. (Plate 34)

Plate 34

In Phoenixville, a pottery of the same name was begun by W. A. Schreiber in 1867. Schreiber produced Rockingham, and the 1870 census indicates there were 20 operatives turning out yellowware and Rockingham valued at $14,223. Even though the pottery appeared to be quite solvent, it was sold in 1882, and Rockingham production was discontinued.

Possibly because of the costs of transporting clay to the potteries, the New York pottery firms were, for the most part, short lived. Both the Poughkeepsie firm of Oncutt & Thompson and the Syracuse firm of Charles W. Manchester & Clark lasted only a year. We know that James Carr's firm in Manhattan made Rockingham for a brief period of time because there exists a marked Rockingham pitcher, however, the firm soon discontinued production of Rockingham.

Other than the Vermont potteries at Bennington, the only New England pottery that can be credited with Rockingham production is the Boston Earthenware Manufactory Company begun by Frederick H. Mear in 1854. William F. Homer owned the property and was a major investor in this East Boston firm even though the name changed several times over the years. Rockingham ware was produced at the Condor Street pottery until it was finally sold in 1876 to Thomas Gray and Lyman W. Clark.

In 1837, a noted Staffordshire potter by the name of James Clews came to the tiny town of Troy, Indiana, with 40 other potters in an ill-advised attempt to recreate the famous English pottery district in

Indiana. Although Rockingham ware was made in Troy, the venture did not succeed because of unskilled workers and the inferior clay of the region which wasn't suited for soft paste pottery production.

When Christopher W. Fenton left Benningtion, Vermont, he relocated in Peoria, Illinois. Here he convinced local backers to fund a huge "departmental pottery" which would produce in addition to stoneware, yellowware, and various forms of brick, a line of Rockingham ware. The manufacture (1859–61) was short lived because of an inadequate market and high production costs.

The production of fruit jars from the Peoria Pottery in Illinois was tremendous (Plate 35), and most of the production is of little interest to the Rockingham collector. But Rockingham glaze was among the many glazes applied to this gracefully shaped stoneware jar. The company was in production from 1872 to 1902, and this shape may be found in various sizes at a much more modest price than canning jars with more traditional glaze applications. (Plate 36)

At the small town of Morton, Illinois, just a few miles south of Peoria, two German emigrants settled and began making field tile. Soon the brothers, Andrew and Barthol Rapp, realized they could fulfill the needs of the local farm women as well as the agronomical needs of their husbands. The enterprising emigrants began making Rockingham ware around 1878 and continued production until 1917.

By the mid 1890s the Rapp Brothers Pottery later known as Morton Pottery was manufacturing Rockingham ware waffle banded mixing bowls, (Plate 37) wine jugs, chamber pots, milk crocks, churns, and pitchers. To make their glaze, finely ground dust from Thames River pebbles was imported and mixed with silica from the Illinois River valley.

Plate 35

Plate 36

37

Plate 37

A price list of late 1800s indicates they made many sizes of oval bakers, fluted rice nappies, plain nappies, bowls and pie plates, all in Rockingham. Three sizes of milk boilers were made. (Plate38) This item was used to clabber milk. By placing it on the back of the wood stove, the whey formed and made cottage cheese. Such ordinary items as plain topped spittoons were made as well as bed pans. Several sizes of a plain jug were made and three sizes of custard cups. A lovely five pint coffee pot was made and a plain individual ½ pint pot as well. The Rapp Brothers Pottery made seven sizes of a Rebecca at the Well teapot, again attesting to the popularity of this design. Several sizes of a globe shaped teapot and a plain individual teapot were made. An ornately designed mug with an indented lambrequin border below the rim and an applied strap handle was produced in addition to a flared sided mug similar to those produced at Bennington (Plate 39), but with a small round handle similar to the one made by McCoy in Ohio.

Plate 38   Plate 39

It's interesting to have descriptions of these pieces because many of them are available at reasonable prices in the Midwest. Six sizes of the waffle banded bowls were made as well as plain undecorated ones. A plain Rockingham flare lipped cuspidor was made as well as an acorn-shaped bank, or money pot as they were earlier called. The tall, slender Rebecca at the Well teapot design was later changed to a squatty globe shape with the design within a relief scroll panel, later a pear-shaped three pint plain jug or pitcher, was added.

To increase sales, around the turn of the century, the Rapp brothers devised a rather unique sales scheme. With a little brochure they described their offer: "We want our customers to act as Agents in and around their neighborhood," it said, "and herewith submit a list of premiums for every Dollar's worth sold. In this way you can supply your kitchen FREE OF CHARGE..." Their offer went on to describe the items a housewife could earn by placing orders from her neighbors. For a $1.00 order she would receive a No. 42 bowl which was the 4½" bowl that is now the most difficult size to find.

Even though pieces from the Rapp Brothers production are not as old as many of those from New Jersey, Vermont, and Maryland, it is still remarkable so many remain in usable condition when we consider most Rockingham ware was used in the kitchen everyday. Housewives of an earlier generation must have been more careful with their dishes, or maybe part of the longevity was in the ware itself. The Rapp Brothers described their pottery as wearing like iron. Even so, and even though each item in my collection is enjoyed every day, I won't pretend they are made of iron and I'll continue to marvel at the pieces without a crack or chip which have come down to us from the caring hands of earlier days. And I will cherish each find as I do this cake pan so it may be passed down once again in perfect, usable condition. (Plate 40).

Plate 40

POTTERS, POTTERIES, AND MARKS

Listed below you will find many known makers of Rockingham. Except where the continuity of a business would be lost, I have listed the manufacturers in chronological order under the town and state. The dates show years of Rockingham production, not the years of the company's operation. Also included are descriptions of the marks used to identify the ware. While not all pieces of this everday ware were marked, the marks described below have been found on pieces of Rockingham. Many of the potteries used several different marks, but if it is not know if they were used on Rockingham I have not included them in this list. To avoid confusion I have listed the names, where known, of the pottery works below the name of the pottery manufactuer.

— CALIFORNIA —

Town: East Oakland
Manufacturer & Date: Daniel Brannon, 1856–57
Pottery Name: Pioneer Pottery

— CONNECTICUT —

Town: Norwich
Manufacturer & Date: Sidney Risley & Son, 1845–81

— DELAWARE —

Town: Hockessin
Manufacturer & Date: Abner Marshall, 1859–66

— ILLINOIS —

Town: Ripley
Manufacturer & Date: John Stout, 1866–69

Town: Morton
Manufacturer & Date: Rapp Brothers Pottery or Morton Earthenware
    Company, 1878–1917
Marks: MORTON/WORKS in circle; POTTERY in center, under the glaze

Town: Peoria
Manufacturer & Date: Christopher Fenton & Decius Clark, 1869–61

— INDIANA —

Town: Troy
Manufacturer & Date: Indiana Pottery Co., 1837–38

— MARYLAND —

Town: Baltimore
Manufacturer & Date: Edwin & William Bennett, 1846–1848
Mark: E & W BENNETT/CANTON/ST Baltimore, impressed

Town: Baltimore
Manufacturer & Date: Edwin Bennett Co., 1848–1938
Mark: E. BENNETT/PATENT/DEC. 2, 1853, impressed

— MASSACHUSETTS —

Town: Boston
Manufacturer & Date: Boston Pottery Co., 1878–1900
Boston Earthenware, 1852–76
Marks: BOSTON/EARTHEN/WARE/MANUF 'G CO, impressed
BOSTON/EARTHENWARE/FACTORY, impressed

— MISSOURI —

Town: Cape Girardeau
Manufacturer & Date: James Post, 1823–33

— NEW JERSEY —

Town: Jersey City
Manufacturer & Date: D. & J. Henderson, 1823–1833
Marks: DJ HENDERSON/JERSEY CITY, impressed in a circle
HENDERSON/FLINTWARE STONEWARE MANUFACTORY,
impressed
HENDERSON'S STONE AND EARTHENWARE MANUFACTORY,
impressed

Town: Jersey City
Manufacturer & Date: American Pottery, 1833–50
Marks: AMERICAN POTTERY MANUFACTURING COMPANY, NEW
JERSEY, printed under glaze inside a flag

Marks: (cont.)
AMERICAN POTTERY MANUFACTURING COMPANY, NEW
JERSEY, under glaze around elliptical design
AMERICAN/POTTERY CO./MANUFACTURING CO. JERSEY
CITY, N.J., letters & numbers 0 1 2 3 4 in relief in circle
AMERICAN/POTTERY/CO./JERSEY CITY in relief, letters and
numbers in circle like previous listing

Town: Perth Amboy
Manufacturer & Date: A. Hall & Son, c. 1866–50

Town: Rahway
Manufacturer & Date: Wm. Turner, c. 1868–70

Town: South Amboy
Manufacturer & Date: John Hancock, 1829–40
Marks: HANCOCK POTTER.

Town: South Amboy
Manufacturer & Date: Abraham Cadmus, 1849–54
Pottery Name: Congress Pottery
Mark: A CADMUS/CONGRESS POTTERY/SOUTH AMBOY/N.J.
with scroll on each side of N.J.

Town: South Amboy
Manufacturer & Date: Hanks & Fish, 1850–52
Pottery Name: Swan Hill Pottery
Mark: HANKS & FISH/SWAN HILL/POTTERY/SOUTH AMBOY, N.J.
in relief under relief swan

Town: South Amboy
Manufacturer & Date: Swan Hill Pottery, James Carr, owner, 1852–54
Mark: SWAN HILL/POTTERY/SOUTH AMBOY, impressed

Town: Trenton
Manufacturer & Date: Taylor & Co., 1852–72
Pottery Name: Trenton Pottery

Town: Trenton
Manufacturer & Date: William Young & Co., 1853–59
Mark: W.H. YOUNG/TRENTON, impressed

Town: Trenton
Manufacturer & Date: Henry Speeler, 1856–79

Town: Trenton
Manufacturer & Date: Excelsior Pottery, 1857–79

Town: Trenton
Manufacturer & Date: J. Mayer, 1860–70
Pottery Name: Arsenal Pottery
Marks: J MAYER/TRENTON impressed in banner/NJ, impressed
FIREPROOF/J. MAYER/TRENTON

Town: Trenton
Manufacturer & Date: John Moses & Son, 1860–90
Pottery Name: Glasgow Pottery

Town: Trenton
Manufacturer & Date: Ott & Co., c. 1863–92

Town: Woodbridge
Manufacturer & Date: Salamander Works, 1825–96
Mark: SALAMANDER WORKS/WOODBRIDGE/N.J. in script,
inscribed in glaze of base
SALAMANDER/WORKS/CANNON STREET/NEW YORK,
impressed office in NY

— NEW YORK —
Town: Huntington
Manufacturer & Date: Brown Brothers, 1863–1904
Marks: BROWN BROTHERS/LONG ISLAND, impressed

Town: Brooklyn (King Co.)
Manufacturer & Date: Cornelius Vaupel, 1878–94

Town: Manhattan
Manufacturer & Date: James Carr & Co., 1856–88

Town: Poughkeepsie
Manufacturer & Date: Oncutt & Thompson Co., 1860–70
Marks: ONCUTT AND THOMPSON/POKEEPSIE, impressed

Town: Syracuse
Manufacturer & Date: Chas. W. Manchester & Fisher W. Clark, 1868–69

Town: Watervaliet
Manufacturer & Date: Wm. E. Warner, 1829–52

— OHIO —

Town: Cincinnati
Manufacturer & Date: George Scott & Son, 1846–1901

Town: Cincinnati
Manufacturer & Date: Samuel Pollack, 1859–74
Pottery Name: The Dayton Street Pottery

Town: Cincinnati
Manufacturer & Date: M. & N. Tempest, 1865–82
Pottery Name: The Dallas Pottery

Town: Liverpool
Manufacturer & Date: Benjamin Harker Sr., 1840–46
    Harker Taylor & Co., 1846–74
Pottery Name: Etruria Pottery
Marks: HARKER/TAYLOR & CO./EAST LIVERPOOL, OHIO, impressed
        on relief circle with propeller-type symbol in center (1846–51)
        ETRURIA WORKS/1862/EAST LIVERPOOL, impressed (c. 1862)
        ETRURIA WORKS/GS HARKER & CO. EAST LIVERPOOL O.,
        impressed

Town: Liverpool
Manufacturer & Date: James Bennett & Bros., 1841–45
Mark: BENNETT & BROTHERS/LIVERPOOL OHIO, impressed

Town: Liverpool
Manufacturer & Date: Salt & Mear, 1841–c.53
Pottery Name: Mansion Pottery
Mark: SALT & MEAR, impressed

Town: Liverpool
Manufacturer & Date: John Goodwin, 1843–53
Pottery Name: Eagle Pottery, Broadway Pottery Works, 1872–75
Mark: J. GOODWIN/1846, impressed

Town: Liverpool
Manufacturer & Date: Goodwin Brothers Pottery Company, 1875–c.85
Pottery Name: Broadway Pottery Works

Town: Liverpool
Manufacturer & Date: Thomas Croxall, 1844–52
Pottery Name: Bennett Pottery

Town: Liverpool
Manufacturer & Date: Vodrey & Woodward, 1847–49

Town: Liverpool
Manufacturer & Date: Woodward, Blakeley & Co. 1848–c. 58
Pottery Name: Phoenix Pottery

Town: Liverpool
Manufacturer & Date: Vodrey & Brother, 1858–76
Pottery Name: Vodrey Pottery or Palissy Works

Town: Liverpool
Manufacturer & Date: Benjamin Harker Jr., 1853–77
Pottery Name: Mansion House Pottery, Wedgewood Pottery

Town: Liverpool
Manufacturer & Date: Knowles, Taylor & Knowles, 1854–1873
Pottery Name: East Liverpool Pottery

Town: Liverpool
Manufacturer & Date: Croxall & Cartwright, 1856–88

Pottery Name: Union Pottery, Mansion Pottery
Mark: CROXALL & CARTWRIGHT/EAST/LIVERPOOL/OHIO,
name in half circle, all in relief

Town: Liverpool
Manufacturer & Date: J.W. Croxall & Son, 1888–1914

Town: Liverpool
Manufacturer & Date: William Brunt Jr., 1860–1874
Pottery Names: Phoenix Pottery, Great Western Pottery Works

Town: Liverpool
Manufacturer & Date: Manley & Cartwright, 1864–72

Town: Liverpool
Manufacturer & Date: Manley, Cartwright & Co., 1872–80

Town: Liverpool
Manufacturer & Date: Cartwright Brothers Pottery Co., 1880–87

Town: Liverpool
Manufacturer & Date: Thompson & Herbert, 1868–70

Town: Liverpool
Manufacturer & Date: C.C. Thompson & Co., 1870–89

Town: Liverpool
Manufacturer & Date: C.C. Thompson Pottery Company, 1889–1917
Mark: Paper label: The C.C. Thompson Pottery Co./manufacturer
of/Semi-Granite/CC. and Decorated Ware/Rockingham and
Yellowware/East Liverpool, Ohio

Town: Liverpool
Manufacturer & Date: Goodwin & Sons Pottery, 1872–80
Pottery Name: Broadway Pottery Works

Town: Liverpool
Manufacturer & Date: Laughlin Brothers, 1873–c. 74

Town: Liverpool
Manufacturer & Date: The Globe Pottery Co., 1882–c. 95

Town: Liverpool
Manufacturer & Date: D.E. McNicol, 1892–1927
Mark: D.E. MCNICOL/EAST LIVERPOOL, OH., impressed

Town: Liverpool
Manufacturer & Date: Syracuse Stoneware Co. (sales office in NY),
1890–c. 96

Town: Liverpool
Manufacturer & Date: Star Pottery, 1875–88
Mark: No mark

Town: Roseville
Manufacturer & Date: Nelson McCoy Pottery, 1916–24
Mark: McCOY

Town: Wellsville
Manufacturer & Date: John Patterson & Sons, 1883–1900
Mark: J PATTERSON/WELLVILLE/OHIO, impressed

Town: Zanesville
Manufacturer & Date: John Howson, 1863–74

Town: Zanesville
Manufacturer & Date: George Pyatt, 1849–79

Town: Zanesville
Manufacturer & Date: Roseville Pottery, 1904–c. 20
Mark: RP Co. on banner

— PENNSYLVANIA —
Town: Philadelphia
Manufacturer & Date: J.E. Jeffords & Co., 1868–70
Marks: FIREPROOF/J.E. JEFFORDS & CO./PHILA./PATENTED
JUNE 28, 1870, impressed
DESIGN PATENTED NOV 13, 1879/L, impressed
WARRANTED/JP/J/CO/PEP/FIREPROOF, stamped in blue
diamond

Town: Philadelphia
Manufacturer & Date: Abraham Miller, 1827–59
Pottery Name: Spring Garden Pottery
Marks: ABRAHAM MILLER, impressed
  ABM, impressed
  MILLER, impressed

Town: Philadelphia
Manufacturer & Date: Isaac Spiegel, Jr., c. 1837–60

Town: Philadelphia
Manufacturer & Date: Yellow Rock, dates unknown
Mark: YELLOW ROCK, stamped in blue or black circle

Town: Phoenixville
Manufacturer & Date: Phoenixville Pottery, c. 1867–92

— VERMONT —

Town: Bennington
Manufacturer & Date: Norton & Fenton, 1844–47
Marks: NORTON & FENTON/BENNINGTON, VT., impressed in a circle
  NORTON & FENTON/EAST BENNINGTON, impressed

Town: Bennington
Manufacturer & Date: Lyman, Fenton & Co., 1847–49
Marks: FENTON'S ENAMEL/PATENTED/Lyman, Fenton & Co./
  BENNINGTON, V.T./1849 4, center, impressed
  Lyman Fenton & Co./ BENNINGTON, Vt, in circle
  Fenton's/ENAMEL/PATENTED/1849, inside circle, impressed
  (This is called the 1849 mark.)
  Fenton's/ENAMEL/PATENTED/1849, within impressed circle,
  date in center
  Fenton's Patent/LYMAN, FENTON & CO., impressed in circle,
  ENAMEL/1849 in center

Town: Bennington
Manufacturer & Date: United States Pottery Co., 1849–58
Marks: UNITED STATES/BENNINGTON Vt., in elliptical line, +/
  POTTERY Co./+, in center, impressed

Town: Bennington
Manufacturer & Date: E. & L.P. Norton, 1861–81
Marks: No mark on Rockingham

Town: Burlington
Manufacturer & Date: Nichols & Co., 1854–60

Town: Burlington
Manufacturer & Date: A.K. Ballard & Co., 1856–72

A GUIDE TO ROCKINGHAM PRICES

Because we have had few definitive directions to pricing many of the different pieces of Rockingham, prices vary to an extreme degree across the country, and even in shops in the same community. Another reason for the difference in pricing across our country is availability. Here in the Midwest I have never seen the large, 3", 8 oz. size custard sell for any less than $40.00, and that was at auction. In the Northwest, I have found these large custards for $25.00 in shops and for much, much less if they have even minor damage.

In a review of price guides over the past 20 years some trends are evident. The prices of common pieces such as bowls have little more than doubled in price. In 1974 a plain 10½" mixing bowl was priced at $35.00. In 1994 this same piece would have a value range of $75.00 to $95.00 across the country. On the other hand, less common pieces such as pie plates have increased in value tripling the 1974 price of $32.50. The same pie plate cannot be purchased for less than $100.00, and in many areas of the country, the price tag is even higher. An undesirable piece for most people, a bedpan was priced at $30.00 in 1974. I saw one in the Ozarks recently for $15.00 and most range between $25.00 and $35.00 even in antique malls close to urban areas where the prices are often highest. For a scalloped shell decorated spittoon priced at $45.00 in 1974 you would expect to pay double this amount, around $100.00 for the same piece today. A Rebecca at the Well teapot sold for $55.00, twenty years later a similar teapot sold for $135.00. Unusual pieces such as a coffee pot with an acorn finial have better than tripled in value. Priced at $160.00 in 1974 the same piece is a lucky find today at $550.00. Fine pieces that are marked or can be attributed to certain potteries have increased the most. A large, 9" hound handled pitcher attributed to a N.J. pottery commanded a price tag of $160.00 twenty years ago, today this same pitcher might go as high as $395.00 to $650.00. From this information it seems evident that as in other commodities, scarcity and demand rule the market. If we are interested in increasing the value of our collections, if we enjoy the appearance of these scarcer, finer items, and if we can afford them, they are good investments.

With all of these things in mind, I have given a rather wide price range for many items to account for availability in different parts of the country.

ROCKINGHAM WARE

Many skills were needed to make the base ware itself. The pottery industry provided employment to men and women alike. *Diorama in the Ceramic Museum, East Liverpool, Ohio.*

Taking wares to the kiln. *Diorama in the Ceramic Museum, East Liverpool, Ohio.*

While tons of pottery was plain and ordinary, the creativity of potters can be seen in the fanciful designs, unique forms, and lustrous glazes which made most everyday items in Rockingham ware a joy to use.

THE COLORS OF
ROCKINGHAM

The gracefully molded yellow clay teapot and the heavy stoneware mug are similarly colored. The butterscotch or caramel hue is the lightest shade of brown found on Rockingham.

A light reddish brown Rockingham glaze, except for one streak, covers the cream pitcher, covers the pie plate with heavy spattering, and drips down the sides of the small bowl with the indented lambrequin border.

These two pitchers, a tall slender domestic product and a traditionally shaped English piece, have a dark reddish glaze not commonly
recognized as Rockingham.

The tall coffee pot is completely covered with dark brown glaze
except for the fine lightly glazed line of the lambrequin border
just below the rim of the pot. The mug, as darkly colored, shows
some of the body, but notice the top of the very dark bottom rim.

Although the dark blue spatters on the interior of this nappy are difficult to detect in the photo, they are there. While it is not usual to see additional color on Rockingham, the Ceramic Museum in Ohio has on display a pitcher made by Bennett and Brothers in the mid-nineteenth century that has green color in addition to the brown of the manganese.

THE GLAZING STYLES OF ROCKINGHAM

The covered pipkin is heavily but sparingly spattered with glaze, leaving the yellow body bare of the glaze on half of its surface. This glazing method is one of the most unusual to find on Rockingham.

The stoneware mug and yellow clay pitcher are covered with a lightly sponged application of glaze. Similarly glazed pieces in the Ohio Ceramic Museum are described as lightly glazed Rockingham.

A fine random spattering of glaze was applied to both the
pie plate and mug. Different amounts of manganese in the
glaze formula or color of the base material can account
for the different shades of brown on the two pieces.

Random, heavy spattering glazed the pie plate and fruit
jar. The heat during firing ran the glaze causing a dripping
design on both pieces. Note the outer edge of the bottom of
the pie plate and the top third of the fruit jar.

The heavy controlled spattering on this pie plate is
thick enough to discern with your fingertips.

A heavy random spattering of glaze darkly
covers the stoneware pitcher and pie plate.

Wiping the glaze from part of the teapot and a portion of the pitcher accents the panel and rib design of both pieces.

The splotchy undefined two-tone glaze found on this pitcher and serving platter was called *tortoise shell* by many of the early potteries.

THE DESIGNS OF
ROCKINGHAM

Even before the phrase *form follows function* was coined, the utilitarian nature of many pottery pieces, such as these three, were designed to perform food preparation and storage duties. Their forms could be contemporary.

Humor dictated the designs for these two flasks — a book and a Toby sitting astride a barrel. Both can be attributed to the pottery in Bennington, Vermont.

Subject matter that tells a story or illustrates nature can be found as decorations on Rockingham pottery. The domestic pitcher on the left depicts wild and tame animals while the English jug on the right tells the story of a fox hunt.

Victorian designs ranged from the simple rendering of drape and bead work which decorates the pitcher with restraint to the large stylized feathers which decorate the Illinois mug.

METHODS OF MAKING
ROCKINGHAM WARE

The simplicity of the design and the visible ridges made by the potter's fingers as he pulled the clay up from the wheel tell us this batter pitcher was hand thrown or made by hand on the wheel.

One of the hundreds of embossed designs made from a mold, this Midwestern pitcher with an applied handle was decorated with berries and leaves.

WHAT ROCKINGHAM IS NOT

Common all over the country, many marked U.S.A., these pudding bowls are spongeware, not Rockingham.

Heavy dark sponging in a distinct pattern completely obliterated the peacock design of this butter crock. However, this crock can be found with a Rockingham glaze.

The pale yellow sponged custard, third from the right, is spongeware. The dark one behind it is Rockingham, as are the small one, second from the left, and the large one directly behind it. The designation of the two remaining custards, the ones on each end, must be a matter of individual judgment.

The two pitchers were made from the same mold design in two different sizes. The larger one on the left is Flint Enamel, while the one on the right is Rockingham. To further muddy the water, I recently saw this same mold design in a size smaller than either of these. The top half was glazed in green, but the bottom definately was Rockingham.

These three bowls were made from the same mold design with a lambrequin border below the rim in two different sizes. The large, pale bowl is alternately sponged with green and brown and is properly called spngeware. The two smaller ones of the same size are glazed very differently, yet both are Rockingham.

Made between 1847 and 1867 by Bennington, this 2¼" octagonal Flint Enamel door knob was also made with a Rockingham glaze.

ROCKINGHAM
FOR THE PANTRY

Wonderful graduations in the depth of color in the Rockingham glaze decorate this ½ gallon stoneware fruit jar from the 1870s. It stands 7¼" tall. $110.00–150.00.

BRANDY PEACHES

Take large white or yellow freestone peaches, not too ripe. Scald them with boiling water and let them stand covered until the water is cold. Do this again, and when they are cold, take them out and lay them on a soft cloth. Cover them with another soft cloth until they are dry. Now put them in stoneware jars and cover them with brandy. Tie paper over the jars and let them stand one week.

For each pound of peaches used, add one pound of sugar to a kettle and one-half pint of water. Bring to a boil and skim the syrup. Put the peaches in and simmer them until they are tender. Pour the brandy from the stoneware jars, put the peaches back in. Mix equal part of syrup and brandy and pour over the peaches. Seal the tops with clean cloth and wax.

The pair of 5½" five cup or 1½ liter fruit jars are usually called brown crocks, not Rockingham. But these two are similar to jars in the collection of the Ceramic Museum in East Liverpool, Ohio, and they are attributed to the 1848–1861 production of the Larkin Brothers in West Virginia. While we cannot give these two this early date, we can clearly and accurately describe them as Rockingham. $12.00–22.00.

Exhibited in the Collection of the Ceramic Museum in East Liverpool, Ohio, this large Rockingham cooler is brown with green streaks in the glaze. It is attributed to Woodward and Vodrey or Vodrey Brothers, 1848–1879. $350.00–500.00.

Left: Made by the thousands by the Peoria Pottery in Illinois in a variety of sizes, this buff stoneware fruit jar was decorated with many different glazes, but this one is Rockingham. It found its way across the United States to Oregon. It stands 6⅞" tall and holds a little over a quart. The two holes on the sides of the top tell us it once had a lid. Marked with impressed PEORIA POTTERY in the unglazed base. Made between 1880 and 1900. $12.00–25.00.

Right: Made in Ohio, maybe as late as 1870, this style of barrel-shaped Rockingham fruit jar was made by many potteries. Holding a half gallon, it stands 7" high. $18.00–35.00.

Standing 6½" high, this Rockingham crock is 8½" in diameter and holds five quarts. It is nicely decorated with two lambrequin borders below a plain band around the top and has two ear handles. It is similar to designs used by the C.C. Thompson Co. in Ohio between 1870 and 1884. $85.00–150.00.

This large 4⅞" high butter crock probably had a lid when it was first purchased, but some did not. Regardless of its covered or uncovered state, this one is nicely designed with a footed base and a narrow double incised band around the top. Attributed to Ohio's production, c. 1890. $65.00–130.00.

The base of this small 4¼" high butter crock is bulbous. Unlike the more common footed design, this crock has very thin walls. Even without their lids, butter crocks are desirable additions to any collection. $75.00–135.00.

ROCKINGHAM
FOR THE KITCHEN

A collection of Rockingham fills a New England dry sink and adds charm to the kitchen.

This 10" high lipless batter jug is a fine example of the potter's art. The graceful ovoid-shaped jug is attributed to the Oregon Pottery Co. in Portland, 1885–1896. $75.00–125.00.

Many marks of use — tiny chips and crazing — show on this 4¼" high, 5½" diameter stoneware kettle with a bail handle and a turned wooden grip. It has a hand rolled lip with a tiny pouring spout, made by the potter's thumb as he finished throwing it on the wheel. The bottom of the kettle rests on six small teardrop-shaped applied feet. The rest of the underside is messy with small pieces of clay that adhered to the kettle during the firing process. $100.00–125.00.

BOILED DANDELIONS

Use the shoots of the first spring dandelions. They are not fit for food after they blossom because they taste bitter. Cut off the roots and throw away any grass or leaves. Rinse well in vinegar water. Put in boiling kettle and cover with boiling water. Add a spoonful of salt and boil slowly for one hour. When they are done, drain most of the liquid off and chop them fine. Add a bit of butter and pepper to taste and serve with a crumbled hard boiled egg.

Most pottery companies that made Rockingham ware produced these oval bakers, and their production lasted well into the first quarter of this century. The large piece is 10¾" long and 8" across while the smaller one is 7" long and 5⅜" across. Both have very dark brown glazes. Large - $100.00–125.00; small - $45.00–65.00.

It is only 4½" high and 6¾" across the lid of this pipkin dating from the 1880s. The glazing on this piece looks as though the potter flung a brush full of glaze over the piece and let it fall sparingly, where it may. This style of bean pot, or pipkin, is always lightly glazed with the Rockingham brown. $250.00–295.00.

This round turn-of-the-century bean pot with handles on each side has a dark tortoise-shell glaze. The flat lid has a mushroom finial. The pot with lid stands 5" tall. $65.00–110.00.

The heavy stoneware body of this 11" diameter Turk's head cake mold is perfect for the slow baking required to make the best Christmas fruit cake or any of your favorite family recipes. $150.00–175.00.

Rich pumpkin color beneath the brown Rockingham glaze makes this 8¾"
diameter redware Turk's head mold especially attractive. I've never had a
crumb out of place as I've tipped a partially cooled poppy seed cake out onto
a large Rockingham pie plate for frosting with lemon icing. $100.00–150.00.

Heavy and durable, this 10½" diameter mixing bowl has seen service in the
kitchen for many years. It's impossible to date or attribute plain working
pieces of Rockingham to any time or place because bowls like this one were
made all over the country for many years. $75.00–95.00.

POPPY SEED CAKE

Grease a large mixing bowl with butter. Mix ¾ lb. of softened butter with two cups of white sugar. Beat four eggs until light and frothy and add to the sugar and butter, mixing well. Mix three cups of flour with a ½ tsp. of salt and 1½ tsp. of baking powder. Put two heaping large spoonfuls of poppy seeds into the flour mixture, and add this to the eggs and sugar evenly with a pint of rich milk. When mixed, add a large coffee cupful of chopped walnuts. Butter and flour a cake mold and bake in a slow oven (325°F) for 1 to 1½ hours.

This mixing bowl and six flared custards were a wedding present in 1925. The bowl measures 8½" diameter and is 3½" high. The little custard is 4¼" across and 2" high. Although these pieces are quite late, the flared design of the custard is hard to find. Mixing bowl - $45.00–65.00; Custard - $20.00–30.00.

No picture could adequately illustrate the size of this massive 14" bowl from the Collection of the Ceramic Museum in East Liverpool, Ohio. Rockingham glaze was applied over the yellow ware banded bowl. $500.00–750.00.

A nest of five plain mixing bowls, all decorated with Rockingham, range in sizes from 10½" down to 6½" in diameter. The largest and the smallest pieces, 14" and 4" diameter, are not commonly found. 10½" - $75.00–95.00; 9¾" - $70.00–$90.00; 8½" - $65.00–85.00; 7¾" - $60.00–80.00; 6½" - $55.00–75.00.

These waffle banded bowls were made by the Rapp Brothers Pottery in Morton, Illinois, between 1878 and 1915. From a 1911 bill of sale, we know they were available in 12 sizes, from 4½" to 15½" in diameter. 6½" - $65.00–85.00; 7½" - $75.00–95.00; 9½" - $95.00–115.00.

This very thin bodied 9½" pie plate is covered with controlled spattering of thick drops of glaze. $95.00–125.00

BIG APPLE PIE

Mix one heaping packed tea cupful of brown sugar with four large spoonfuls of flour and a large pinch of salt in a small stew pan. Pour a tea cupful of water over this and mix well. Add another half of cupful of water and cook until it thickens, stirring it all the time so it won't stick or lump. Take it off the range and add two large spoonfuls of butter and a bit of vanilla. Make enough paste (pastry) for a big pie and slice three big sour apples (Gravenstein or Macintosh) onto the bottom paste and pour the cooked syrup over them and put on the top paste. Bake in a hot oven (400°F) for about 40 minutes.

The largest of these pie plates is just under 12" in diameter, and all pieces are completely glazed on both sides. They were made over a period of 60 years by many potteries from across the nation. 11¾" - $125.00–155.00; 11" - $120.00–150.00 each.

It's easy to see the difference of color and the different textures of the glazes on this assortment of pie plates which range in size from 9½" to 11½" in diameter. $110.00–135.00 each.

In his book on the Bennington potteries, Barrett called this large size, wide squatty pitcher, a mixing pitcher. Although of different proportions than the 4" high, 6" diameter one made in Vermont, this one is 4½" high by 5½" in diameter, it appears similar with the rolled rim and footed base. $55.00–70.00.

Darkly glazed, the banded milk boiler is 4½" tall and of equal diameter. It can be attributed to the Rapp Brothers Pottery in Morton, Illinois. $45.00–60.00.

Milk boilers were used to make cottage cheese, and the dark stains on the bottom of this piece attest to its years of use on a wood stove. This one is 3¾" high and 4½" in diameter. $40.00–55.00.

CURD (Cottage Cheese)

Set the old milk in the boiler at the back of the range until it clabbers. Don't let it boil. After supper, leave the oven door open and set the boiler on the door turning it frequently, cutting it with a knife as it sets. Stir it gently now and then, keeping it just as hot as the finger will bear. When the whey shows all around the curd, put all of it in a coarse bag and hang it in a cool place for three to four hours or overnight. When ready, turn from the bag and chop as finely as wanted. Dress with salt and pepper or with sugar, sweet cream, and a little nutmeg.

A heavy Rockingham glaze covers this tea kettle with a wood and wire bailed handle. Below the kettle's top rim is a beautifully modeled band of shells interspersed with a spearpoint decoration. Even the base of the applied spout is decorated with a reversed shell. The shallow domed lid has another row of spearpoints around the base of the mushroom-shaped finial. The most unique kettle detail is the small brass device on the handle which keeps the lid from tipping off. Two yellow ware kettles of the same embossed design but decorated with printed floral designs instead of Rockingham are in the Collection of the Ceramic Museum of East Liverpool, Ohio. They are attributed to Knowles, Taylor, and Knowles, c. 1871. $225.00–395.00.

A rich reddish brown glaze completely covers both sides of this large nappy which measures 13½" in diameter and 3½" high. $165.00–225.00.

PIGEON PIE

Kill and pluck four wild pigeons. Cut them into halves and put them into a baking pan. Baste them with melted butter while they bake in a hot oven for 45 minutes. Continue to baste with butter every 10 minutes. Line a large nappy with butter paste (pastry). Dice a pound of ham and slice six hard boiled eggs into separate bowls. Put a layer of pigeon on the bottom paste; salt and pepper to taste. Layer with ham and then with sliced eggs. Continue to layer until all ingredients are used. Make a gravy from the drippings in the roasting pan and pour over the pie. Cover the top with a layer of paste. From the scraps, cut out fanciful leaves and flowers and decorate the top around a vent hole cut in the middle. Bake in a hot oven for about 30 minutes until the paste is done.

The largest nappy is 10½" across and the two smaller ones are 8¼" and 6¾". The 10½" and 6¾" pieces have embossed feet on the bottom. 10½" - $100.00–125.00; 8¼" - $75.00–95.00; 6¾" - $65.00–85.00.

This assortment of custards range from being lightly to heavily glazed. The two heavily glazed pieces on the right have been attributed to John Patterson and Sons of Ohio. The three large pieces in the middle hold eight ounces. On the left, the more common, small custards hold six ounces. Patterson - $18.00–22.00 each; 8 oz. - $25.00–45.00; 6 oz. - $12.00–22.00.

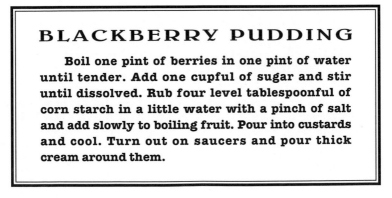

BLACKBERRY PUDDING

Boil one pint of berries in one pint of water until tender. Add one cupful of sugar and stir until dissolved. Rub four level tablespoonful of corn starch in a little water with a pinch of salt and add slowly to boiling fruit. Pour into custards and cool. Turn out on saucers and pour thick cream around them.

These large 3" high custards are more easily found in the far West than in the Midwest. These are heavily glazed over thick bodies. Others are more lightly decorated on thinner walled custards. $25.00–45.00 each.

Similar in both size and form, pitchers like these did kitchen duty across this country for many years. The mold design of the darkly glazed pitcher on the left is similar to one used by the Red Wing Pottery of Minnesota, c. 1910. The lightly glazed pitcher is of an earlier vintage and possibly from Ohio or Illinois. Heavily glazed - $45.00–75.00; lightly glazed - $75.00–125.00.

ROCKINGHAM
FOR THE TABLE

J. Mayer made this finely modeled 6¼" high stoneware pitcher at his
Arsenal Pottery in Trenton, New Jersey, c. 1860. A 9¼" pitcher, with
the same two-sided anchor and chain design with a rope design just
below the lip and an applied handle on the pear-shaped body, was
exhibited in a show of early New Jersey pottery in 1947 at the
Newark Museum. The bottom of this pitcher is almost completely
covered with a large 3" wide, 2" high, impressed mark which reads:
J. MAYER; TRENTON; N.J. Mayer's - $395.00–650.00; unmarked -
$225.00–295.00.

Peacocks preen and strut among the palm trees on this 8" high heavy pitcher. While pitchers of this design are often classified as spongeware, the Ceramic Museum in East Liverpool, Ohio, exhibits a pitcher and butter crock in the same design. The pitcher is described as a molded Rockingham storage vessel in a light glaze, attributed to C.C. Thompson Pottery Company, 1870–1884. $125.00–195.00.

Contemporary and hand thrown, this beautifully designed 5" high milk pitcher was made in Sweden by Hoganas Ceramics, c. 1940. While it is a wonderful example of the potter's art, the design could never be confused with earlier wares made in this country. $30.00–45.00.

The dark iridescent lustre, clearly visible as bluish-purple lights on the lower third of this early 7½" high, 1½-pint pitcher, almost obliterates the modeling details of a horned cow's head within an embossed flower scroll. The belled cow's head decorates both sides of the pitcher. $175.00–295.00.

It is unusual to find the delicate details, like the restrained drape and bead design on the neck of this lightly glazed, 6½" tall pitcher from the 1880s, not obliterated by thick glaze. Under close inspection, we can see undissolved specks of the manganese oxide used to glaze this piece. $165.00–225.00.

Brush marks indicating the method used to apply the glaze on this large 8½",
1½-gallon pitcher are clearly visible on the inside of the wide lip. An oval
wreath of leaves and hanging game (rabbits, ducks, geese, turkeys, and
grouse) decorate both sides. The top of the handle is decorated with a large
four-petaled flower. Made in many different sizes in the Midwest, c. 1890.
$175.00–250.00.

A beautifully modeled iris decorates
the body of this tall 8¾" slender
pitcher. A pointed four-petaled
flower band is set just below the
rim, and the base is rounded and
ribbed. A common find in the Midwest, this dark reddish glazed piece
was made c. 1900. Other flower
designs, such as peonies, may be
found on similarly shaped and
glazed pitchers. $75.00–125.00.

Impressed on the bottom with the word "ROCKINGHAM," this twentieth-century English pitcher was made by Arthur Wood and Son Ltd. in the Staffordshire district of England. The firm has been in business since 1904. Pitchers with this same design depicting a horse race on the traditionally shaped early body with a horse's head on the applied handle can be found marked with "ARTHUR WOOD; ENGLAND." $95.00–150.00.

Graceful in design and pattern, this pitcher stands 8½" tall. the allegorical pattern of two young lads feeding a goat covers both sides of the pear-shaped body. $175.00–250.00.

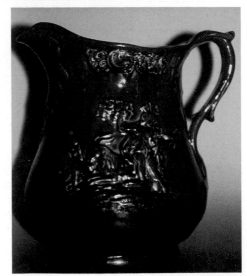

A hanging turkey decorates one side of this 6¾" high pitcher attributed to the work of A. Hall and Sons at their Perth Amboy, NJ, pottery. The other side of this c. 1870 pitcher is decorated with a running stag. The handle on this piece is a rustic design. A large 10" high presentation pitcher with this same design was exhibited in a 1949 pottery show at the Newark Museum. $250.00–350.00.

Larger than the piece above, this 9" pitcher is also attributed to A. Hall and Sons. The pitcher's handle is different from the one exhibited in the 1949 show. Early potters commonly made small changes in their designs, using different handles on the same molded body. The nose of the hound handle, called a dog handle by the nineteenth century potters, is short and rests on the rim of the pitcher. Unlike the design from the Bennington, Vermont, production and those of Harker in Ohio, the throat of the dog's head on this New Jersey piece rests completely on the dog's forelegs with no space in between. $395.00–650.00.

A running stag with a wide set of horns decorates the other side of the pear-shaped pitcher, also illustrated in the photo at the bottom of page 90. $395.00–650.00.

A simple design of panel and ribs decorates this 7½" tall pitcher. The narrow, 3½" neck makes this piece appear much taller than its actual height. Marked with an incised M&E, it is the work of Mayer & Elliot of the English Staffordshire district. Made in 1860, this ware that was named Rockingham is now called "treacle ware" in England. $195.00–295.00.

Heavy and functional, this early, hand-thrown, one-quart teapot with a flat lid and button finial will still do its duty. Found in a Missouri flea market, the hand crafting, the concentric ridges of clay, can be felt on the inside of the pot. The outside was smoothed as it turned on the wheel for a nice finish. Simple pieces such as these are often regarded as brown ware by collectors and dealers alike, but the Ceramic Museum in Ohio exhibits a similar, plainly designed teapot attributed to the Baggot Brothers Pottery, 1850–1896, and calls it Rockingham. $25.00–45.00.

One of the most gracefully designed teapots is this 7¼" high pot with a simple design and topped by a small flower finial. Believed to be made in Illinois or Ohio, c. 1870. $85.00–150.00.

The Rockingham glaze was cleaverly applied to this rib and panel teapot. The simple geometric design of the body and lid are relieved by ornate scrolls on the applied handle and spout. It is 6⅞" high to the top of the flower finial on the shallow dome lid. $85.00–130.00.

Below: The base of the rib and panel teapot has five embossed teardrop-shaped feet. Other embossed feet can be found in the shapes of hearts and flowers, we know that the Rockingham pieces made in the Bennington pottery were never made with these embossed feet.

Made first in the Baltimore firm of the Bennett Pottery from a Coxon design, the Rebecca at the Well teapot became one of the most popular Rockingham items. Made by many potteries across the country, yet one was never made in Bennington, Vermont. Neither of these teapots carry the inscription below the design, but many do. The large 10" pot with the high domed lid topped by an ornate finial is similar in design to one produced by the D.E. McNichol Pottery Co. of Ohio. They made their Rockingham until 1927. The smaller 1½-pint teapot has nicer modeling details and sharper paneling. The applied spout is decorated with scrolls, and the small domed lid is covered with an inverted lambrequin border below the mushroom-shaped finial Both pieces were probably made in one of the many Ohio firms. 10" - $155.00–185.00; 1½ pint - $85.00–125.00.

Just 3¾" high to its lidless top, this individual teapot was made from a two-part mold. It is marked with the barely legible incised mark of the Dalta Pottery. The piece was found in a Sunday flea market in Bristish Columbia. $3.00–5.00.

Two darkly glazed pieces, the heavy body of the 10¼" high pear-shaped coffee pot is relieved by its curvilinear design. The stark simplicity of this piece is broken only by the lambrequin border below the top rim, the finger grips on the applied handle, and the tall acorn-shaped finial. The large sugar bowl is marked with a P within a circle in relief, but the pottery is still unknown. It stands 6" high. A leaf shape decorates the applied ear-shaped handles on the linear eight-paneled body below the paneled lid with a flower finial. Coffee pot - $450.00–575.00; sugar bowl - $250.00–325.00.

This tiny 1¼" diameter, 4" high, individual creamer was made in Glasgow, Scotland, by the Port Dundas Pottery Company. A miniature lip allows pouring from the small short neck of this stoneware piece heavily covered with Rockingham glaze. The oval mark is impressed in the unglazed base. This mark was used on Rockingham during the 1870s. This piece was found in a dig in the English Yorkshire district. $50.00–65.00.

This simple 4" high pitcher from the production of the East Liverpool, Ohio, area is typical of pieces transported by water or rail throughout the country from this large production area in the late 1800s. Although tons of Rockingham ware were produced in Ohio, the small cream pitchers are very hard to find. $95.00–125.00.

The mold design of this 4⅝" cream pitcher is more commonly seen in blue and white spongeware and white ware. Dating from c. 1880, the scroll details on the shoulder of the wide base are almost completely obliterated by the heavy application of Rockingham glaze. They can be barely felt with the fingertips. $75.00–125.00.

Tall and slender, gently flaring to the wider base, this 5" cream pitcher's form is similar to the form of creamers in semi-vitreous and hard paste china of the late nineteenth century. When we are without definite information about a piece, often the design on the mold or the shape of the piece itself will offer us a clue. $50.00–75.00.

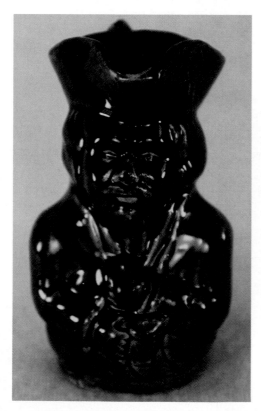

The face of "Sir Toby Belch" on this cream pitcher was commonly seen on American tables after c. 1850. We call them "Tobys" today, and this one is very similar to a mold design used at Bennington. Both are 5⅝" high, but this one, which was found in England, has a deeply concave base, and the Bennington Toby has a flat, completely glazed base. $95.00–140.00.

97

Any outsize piece of Rockingham, whether very large or very small, is a real treasure. The diminutive 4" high sugar bowl with the embossed daisy decorations, ribbed lid, and the tiny finial is a real find. Even the small ear handles are formed into a decorative leaf design. $250.00–350.00.

Hand thrown on the potter's wheel, this 5" tall mug has a dark Rockingham glaze over the heavy stoneware body. The handle is thick and heavy, c. 1890. $45.00–65.00.

The darkly glazed mug on the left of this 4¼" tall pair belies the statement that all darkly glazed Rockingham is of an early vintage. The shape of the flower decal, which decorated these around 1930, is still visible on the mug on the right. These mugs were made in sets with a tall cylindrical pitcher. $18.00–25.00.

The shape of a simple flared mug with a strap handle is a favorite shape of many collectors. Similar mugs were made in Vermont, New Jersey, Maryland, Pennsylvania, and of course, Ohio and Illinois, from about 1850 to 1900. The four pictured here range in size from 3¼" to 3⅞" tall. $95.00–135.00 each.

Only the outside of this heavy, 4½" tall, stoneware mug, which dates to c. 1870, was lightly glazed with Rockingham, as are similarly decorated pieces in the East Liverpool, Ohio, museum. $75.00–125.00.

This ornate 5" mug was originally described as a feather pattern by the Rapp Brothers Pottery in Morton, Illinois, in the late 1800s. Later the mug was described as having a leaf design. Not as popular with many Rockingham ware enthusiasts, these mugs may still be found at nominal prices. I can visualize a holiday buffet set with these holding hot spiced cider. $18.00–22.00.

This is another design of a 5" mug made by the Rapp Brothers in Illinois. Decorated with parrots, lattice, and leaves, its design is more reminiscent of the Gulf States and warm lanais rather than the cold Midwest where it was conceived in the late 1800s. $12.00–18.00.

There is no doubt of the time frame that produced this Midwestern mug of the early 1930s. $20.00–35.00.

These very heavy bowls from c. 1900 have a ribbed embossed band that can be found in several sizes. The large bowl is only 2½" high and 7" in diameter and weighs slightly over two pounds. 7" - $50.00–65.00; 6½" - $35.00–50.00.

This 8½" diameter fluted rice nappy can be attributed to the Rapp Brothers Morton Pottery works in Illinois. Their 1911 price list showed the rice nappy which they made in six sizes ranging from 6½" in diameter to a large 11" one. $85.00–110.00.

The French firm of Hautin & Boulanger made this Rockingham fruit plate c. 1880. It is 8" across its thin, finely made surface. It is embossed with a design of beautifully detailed berries and leaves. $35.00–65.00.

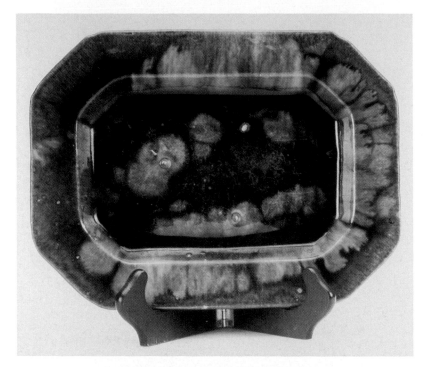

This 8¼" by 10¾" octagonal platter may be found in several sizes. We know from a similar yellow ware platter in the Ceramic Museum Collection in Ohio that the design was made by Bennett & Brothers early in the 1840s. The tortoise shell style Rockingham glaze is especially attractive. $250.00–325.00.

The Lyman Fenton Co. in Bennington, Vermont, made this 9" long, 8⅝" wide serving plate in Rockingham, sometime between 1849 and 1858. Some of these pieces bear a particularly lustrous glaze due to a procedure used by Fenton. After the bisque firing, a glossy underglaze was applied. This more costly and time-consuming procedure was abandoned between 1856 and 1860. The design with its graceful scrolls and ribbed corner panels is especially charming. $125.00–150.00.

Ten inches high to the top of the fruit finial sitting atop a trio of serrated leaves, this 12" long covered casserole would hold enough food for a large family. Wide center panels are interspersed with two narrow panels on the base and the domed lid. The applied handles have survived without a chip. The color of the body of this piece is a rich pumpkin color which gives the Rockingham glaze added excitement. $550.00–750.00.

MISCELLANEOUS
ROCKINGHAM FOR THE HOME

The use of early pottery is usually associated with the traditional country style of decorating. The simple 1857 Missouri pine cupboard houses an entertainment center. More importantly, a collection of Rockingham is combined with a collection of Indian baskets, small rugs, and powder horns. Not only does the warmth of color and the substantial feel of the Rockingham enhance this focal point of the room, but the designs on the two pitchers on the top shelf, the leaping stags combine with and accent the Western look popular today.

Completely covered with a dark glaze, this shoe flask is 6½" tall and 7¼" long. It holds a liter which surely makes it a product from an English pottery. $125.00–200.00.

E. A. Barber, the revered ceramic scholar from the nineteenth century, said that the figural work done at Bennington could be attributed to Daniel Greatbach. This 8" bottle with "Toby" sitting astride a barrel which carries the words OLD TOM can be attributed to the Bennington output and was made between the years 1849 and 1858. $350.00–450.00.

Pictures can't convey the exquisite detail of a finely crafted book flask. The mold details on this pint flask include the stitching along the spine of the book as well as lines indicating separate pages. The potter's humor is in evidence in the inscribed words, DEPARTED SPIRITS. A lustrous glaze covers the entire book. It can be attributed to Bennington's production. $300.00–400.00.

Made in England in this century by Arthur Wood and Sons, this Rockingham marked jug is 7½" high. The embossed design has a bust of a hunt master on the front and the hunters on horseback with their hounds on the back. Symbols of the hunt, a horn, a fox head, and running hounds, decorate the very bottom, but the outstanding detail of the jug is the wonderfully modeled fox handle. The fox is slightly crouched with his tail down and the space between his belly and the jug gives good purchase for three fingers. $150.00–200.00.

Standing 8½" to its lidless top, this thick walled ale jug dates from c. 1880. The head of the hound handle was broken off years ago, and the piece was barely rescued from a junk pit. Even without its lid and in damaged condition this 5½ quart beer container is a collector's find, and it looks great filled with fall mums. Damaged - $35.00–50.00; perfect - $250.00–350.00.

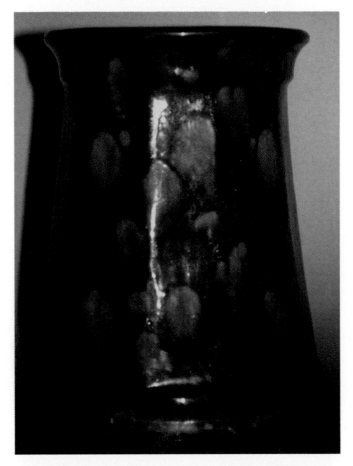

Large splotches of the type of glaze aptly called tortoise shell, decorate this 9" tall paneled humidor with a flare top. $75.00–100.00.

The flare base of this tobacco humidor provides weight to the tall fluted columnar shape. Even without its lid this 7" high piece is a desirable addition to a Rockingham collection. $65.00–90.00.

This richly glazed shell-patterned spittoon is 6½" across the top and can be attributed to the Ohio production of Harker before 1879. $85.00–100.00.

A collector's treasure even without its saucer, this 4" tall Rockingham flower pot dates to the 1880s. $50.00–75.00.

The embossing on the front vase is filled with glaze obscuring the detail. It's 5½" tall and is 7½" wide and dates to the 1890s. Popular in the early 1900s the taller one is 8¼" high. Both vases are attributed to an Ohio or Midwestern pottery. 5½" - $25.00–50.00; 8¼" - $45.00–65.00.

A large applied leaf decorates this 8" tall vase. Like many older pieces of simple design, this piece from around 1910 could have been made today. $30.00–45.00.

Miniature and in perfect detail, this tiny 3" churn still retains its lid and dasher. $75.00–125.00.

This miniature churn, missing its lid, is completely covered with a dark glaze. $10.00–15.00.

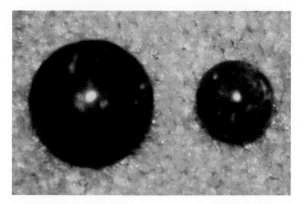

The potters often made toys for their children. These two Rockingham marbles were found among a grandfather's cache. $8.00–15.00.

This money pot, as it might have been called by the potter who made it, or stoneware bank is 4" high to the top of the pointed finial and 3½" across. Its base still retains the marks which show where the potter cut it from the wheel. $40.00–65.00.

ROCKINGHAM FOR THE BATH AND SICKROOM

Any Rockingham shaving mug is a real treasure. This unique, 4¾" high mug tells the story of a man's maturation, the three stages of man. First we see the open smiling face of a youth with a banded cap. Next, (shown on the next page) he grows and joins the work force and wears his billed cap with straightforward determination and under it, his face is set in grim resolve. As we turn the mug to the third side, we see again a smiling face (shown on page 121). But this is a mature face, happy with retirement, with his glasses pushed up on his forehead. This wonderful piece, marked C & E, was found in an old trunk. It really was! Cork and Edge were potters in Burslem in the Staffordshire district of England between 1846 and the 1860s. Other ineligible lettering extends around the rim of the base, but it is so filled with glaze it is indecipherable even with photography. $500.00–650.00.

The oval, paneled 6½" long soap dish in the rear of the photo is indented on both of its long sides giving it a graceful shape. The smaller one in front is also paneled. It's 5⅜" long and 2⅜" high. 6½" - $85.00–100.00; 5⅜" - $75.00–95.00.

SOAP

Boil for six hours 10 gallons of lye made from green wood ashes. Add 10 pounds of grease and fats saved from the kitchen. Don't use rancid grease or fat. If it is ropy looking, add more lye until the grease is absorbed. Dissolve a quart of salt in ½ gallon of hot water and add it to the soap in the kettle. Keep the soap boiling for 20 minutes. Take off the fire and when cool, cut into cakes.

This very large soap dish is 7¼" long and 3¼" high. A dark glaze covers this piece which was probably made in the Midwest around 1880. $120.00–150.00.

This could have been a tourist's keepsake from England. The 4¼" high bottle was fitted with a cork inside the neck and plugged with a daintily turned wooden stopper used to hold scent for a lady. $20.00–45.00.

Among the items made for the sick room, a bedpan with a Rockingham glaze was made by many potteries across the country into the late 1800s. $15.00–35.00.

BIBLIOGRAPHY

Barber, Edwin Atlee. *The Pottery and Porcelain of the United States: An Historical Review of American Ceramic Art from the Earliest Times to the Present Days.* New York and London: G. P. Putnam's Sons, 1893; combined with Marks of American Potters and reprinted, New York: Feingold & Lewis, 1976.

Barrett, Richard Carter. *Bennington Pottery and Porcelain.* New York: Bonanza Books, Division of Crown Publishing, 1958.

——*How to Identify Bennington Pottery: Easy Photo Guide to Detail & Variety.* Brattleboro, Vermont: The Stephen Greene Press, 1964.

Eaglestone, Arthur A. & T. A. Lockett. *The Rockingham Pottery.* Rutland, Vermont: Charles E. Tuttle Company Inc.

Garth's Auctions Inc., Delaware, Ohio

Gates, William C. Jr. & Dana E. Ormerod. *The East Liverpool, Ohio, Pottery District.* California, Pennsylvania: The Society for Historical Archaeology, 1982.

Godden, Geoffrey A. *British Pottery and Porcelain 1780-1850.* A. S. Barnes and Company, Inc.

Hall, Doris and Burdell. *Morton's Potteries: 99 Years: a Product Guide.* Nixa, Missouri: A & J Printers, 1982.

Ketchum Jr., William C. *The Pottery and Porcelain Collectors Handbook: a Guide to Early American Ceramics from Maine to California.* New York: Funk & Wagnalls, 1971.

——*American Country Pottery, Yelloware & Spongeware.* New York: Alfred A. Knopf, 1987.

Kovel, Ralph M. and Terry H. *Dictionary of Marks: Pottery and Porcelain.* New York: Crown Publishers, Inc. 1953.

——*New Dictionary of Marks: Pottery & Porcelain, 1850 to the Present.* New York: Crown Publishing Inc. 1986.

——*Antique Price Guide.* 1975–76; 1976–77; 1981–82.

Leibowitz, Joan. *Yellow Ware: the Transitional Ceramic.* Box E. Exton, Pennsylvania: Schiffer Publishing Ltd. 1985.

McAllister, Lisa S. & John L. Michel. *Collecting Yellow Ware: an Identification & Value Guide.* Paducah, Kentucky: Collector Books, Division of Schroeder Publishing Co.

McCabe, Carol. *Collecting Yellow Ware.* Harrisburg, Pennsylvania: Historical Times Inc. 1984.

McConnell, Kevin. *Spongeware and Spatterware.* Pennsylvania: Schiffer Publishing Ltd. 1990.

The Pottery and Porcelain of New Jersey, 1688-1900. An exhibition catalogue, April 8–May 11, 1947, from the Newark Museum.

The Pottery and Porcelain of New Jeresey, Prior to 1876. An exhibition catalogue, February 1 to March 20, 1915, The Newark Museum Association.

Schroeder's Antiques Price Guide, 1994, 12th Edition. Paducah, Kentucky: Collector Books, 1994.

Thorn, C. Jordan. *Handbook of Old Pottery and Porcelain Marks.* New York: Tudor Publishing Co. 1947.

Wallace. *Homestead Price Guide.* 1978.

Warman's Antiques and their Prices. Elkins Park, Pennsylvania: Warman Publishing Co. Inc. 1974; 1976–77.